Networking
Fundamentals

Networking Fundamentals

Joseph Levy
Glenn Hartwig

MIS:
PRESS

A Subsidiary of
Henry Holt and Co., Inc.

First Edition—1995

Printed in the United States of America.

1-55828-404-4

10 9 8 7 6 5 4 3 2 1

MIS:Press books are available at special discounts for bulk purchases for sales promotions, premiums, fund-raising, or educational use. Special editions or book excerpts can also be created to specification.

For details contact: Special Sales Director
                         MIS:Press
                         a subsidiary of Henry Holt and Company, Inc.
                         115 West 18th Street
                         New York, New York 10011

Editor-in-Chief: Paul Farrell

Managing Editor: Cary Sullivan

Technical Editor: Wayne Rash

Copyedit Manager: Shari Chappell

Copy Editor: Gwynne Jackson

Development Editor: Judy Brief

Production Editor: Stephanie Doyle

Dedication

For my Brother, Harold.

—Joe Levy

For the radiant Daphne and the wondrous Theone.

—Glenn Hartwig

Table of
Contents

Chapter 3: A Basic LAN Cabling Tool Kit 61

Chapter 10: Why Is Imaging Popular? **165**

Chapter 11: Sharing Storage Areas and Programs **176**

Appendix A: User Groups and Other LAN Resources 211

Appendix B: Computer Magazines 219

Appendix C: A Sample Request for Proposal 223

Appendix D: LAN Vendors 227

Appendix E: The Internet 231

Acknowledgments

Thanks to my co-author, Glenn Hartwig, my technical editor, Wayne Rash, and my editor at MIS:Press, Judy Brief, for making this book possible.

—Joe Levy

Introduction

Though many feel trepidation when facing the prospect of understanding and using *local area networks* (LANs), the jump into the LAN world isn't as daunting as you might expect. Much of what you already know will serve you well when you explore the brave new world of LANs.

If, at this point, you still feel a little afraid, don't worry: you're not alone. As Kris Jamsa pointed out in *Welcome to...Personal Computers* (another book from MIS: Press), "If you are like most people, just the thought of learning about computers is scary. You probably already have enough stress in your life without worrying about computers." The temptation is to think that LANs are even more stressful. After all, a LAN is more complicated, consisting of two or more computers, software, connecting hardware, cabling, and assorted peripherals. All this is true, but remember, there's a logical consistency to LANs, just as with personal computers. Once you get a handle on the terminology and on the way all the pieces fit together, getting to know LANs is logical, consistent, and reliable.

Ultimately, we'd like you to treat this book as a knowledgeable friend who not only can help you get over your fears and apprehensions but can help you on your way to gaining real expertise. Although individual products are discussed in detail in some chapters, most of the book emphasizes the big picture.

Along the way, you might even find out that you don't need a LAN at all. That is fine; we're not trying to sell you anything. In fact, this book is designed to present fresh information on hardware and software alternatives to LANs. Chapter 10, for example, is devoted to nothing but alternatives to LANs.

LANs are Technical

LANs are a technical phenomena made up of two sets of basic components that work in harmony:

- The *physical network* includes all the hardware, from computers to cables and connectors.

- The *logical network* includes what LAN users see on their screens and printers, the services available to users and managers, and the software that contains the instructions that let the hardware function as a network.

Sometimes the jargon can get complicated, and LAN managers seem like they are talking a language all their own. However, we have included glossaries at the end of each chapter to keep you from feeling overwhelmed as you learn the basics. We've also included a complete glossary in the appendix section for easy reference at any time.

Although the focus of this book is LANs, it also touches upon some of its close cousins, particularly metropolitan area networks (MANs) and wide area networks (WANs), which are designed to span entire cities, countries, or continents. LANs, however, have their own unique characteristics that make them different from other networks. This book explains these differences in detail.

By reading this book, we're confident that you will find that learning about LANs is really quite easy. Our goal isn't to turn you into a LAN administrator, or launch you into a new career. Instead, we'll make you comfortable with the idea of LANs, then throw in some guidance to help you work with them. Each chapter is brief, designed to take only from 15 minutes to an hour of your time.

Who Should Read This Book?

If you just bought a second or third PC and are thinking about linking them, or perhaps you've heard that you're getting a LAN at work, this book is for you. People looking to buy their first LAN should find the buyer's guide information especially helpful. In just a few minutes you'll get to know LANs and what makes them work for people just like you. We'll include contact and buyer information on LAN products and LAN-related products and services to help you take the next steps.

A History of LANs

When you speak of a Local Area Network (LAN) today, you are generally thinking of a collection of desktop PCs connected to computers designated as servers by some type of wire. In offices as well as factories, LANs let people quickly broadcast typed messages, and share data storage areas and printers among their group.

However, to get to that point, LANs and supporting technologies have evolved considerably. Long before there were LANs there was the *mainframe*, a large, powerful, central computer. The earliest modern computers dating back to the 1950s fell into this class. Many occupied entire buildings. People who wanted to use a mainframe often had to submit requests to computer operators who encoded elaborate instructions on punch cards. And then the person making the request waited hours, even days, for results. Worse, if someone made a mistake, watch out! A single miscoded card would mean that the user would have to resubmit the entire program.

Mainframe computer manufacturers eventually added terminals so people could submit requests on their own, from their desks, without having to physically go where the computer was located and without having to seek the intercession of the computer operator. Terminals look much like ordinary PCs, complete with keyboards and screens, but can only work when connected to a larger computer. In the 1970s smaller mainframes, called *minicomputers*, became popular. With the advent of "minis," companies could buy a half-dozen smaller, but nonetheless very powerful, computing machines for considerably less than a million-dollar mainframe.

Getting the Minis Back Together

Different departments of many computer-using companies were happy to have their own minicomputers. Freed from the mainframe, each group could customize its own mini's behavior to its own requirements. But this created a new problem: how to quickly recombine the data from the separate computers?

Several large corporate computer users, and government agencies such as the U.S. Department of Defense, began cabling their minicomputers back together. Thus were born the first functional computer networks; the continued need for networking has changed the computer industry and computer use forever. To some extent computer companies were forced to publicize the secrets of their computers' operation so that people could connect them in a network with a competitor's machine.

Software That Talks Back

As the minis got smaller and cheaper, the possibility arose that only one person might use any given computer at any given time. Computer companies had to entertain the notion that computer users might not feel particularly thrilled about having to learn how to program a computer just to use it and might not be particularly charmed by the prospect of having to wait hours or days for the computer to deliver the results of a query. Beyond this, of course, was the growing recognition that computers were enormously useful tools. More and more people wanted the kinds of information and analysis computers could provide, and more and more computer companies realized that making computers easier to use was essential if they wanted to tap into the enormous wealth that could be garnered from this burgeoning demand. Suddenly, it became mandatory for computer manufacturers and software producers alike to write *interactive software*, programs that responded immediately to user commands. This was a radical idea in its day but it just goes to show you how much our conception of computers has changed. Today, a computer that needs to be approached with specialized knowledge is a rarity, and computers that don't respond in thousandths of a second are likely on their way to the scrap heap.

Enter Personal Computers

Then came the rise of PCs in the 1980s. PCs offered processing and storage capacity equivalent to larger systems that were just a few years older. They could fit on individual desktops. As PCs proliferated, so did products designed to enhance their productivity. Some of these products, however, were too expensive for each PC user to have. Still, they were beneficial for everyone to have. Hard drives, for example, offered fast access to large amounts of permanent magnetic storage, but even relatively small ones cost over $3,000 in 1983.

A small company in Utah responded that year with one of the first reliable PC file servers, called a *disk server*. Novell, Inc. prospered and came to dominate the first decade of PC LANs. Even then their LAN software not only shared files, but offered a simple way to store larger files than any standard PC could handle. Today many network vendors offer equivalent features, often at less cost. But it will take some time for the industry-wide feeling that Novell is "the only game in town" to wear off.

File servers have evolved in the last decade. Some systems can make backup copies of data without halting user programs. Many file servers can be installed to share your current hard disks without any changes to the disk's layout. High-end systems now store data on multiple hard drives, switching disks automatically if one should fail.

All things being equal, Novell LANs are usually quite fast but also tend to be at the high end of the price scale. If raw speed is not your highest priority, you're in luck. There are numerous other ways to share computer resources (as we'll discover in the course of this book), and many of them may be perfectly adequate to your needs. If that is the case, you may be able to save yourself some money by considering LAN alternatives.

Printer-sharing features have been available on LANs for years. LAN print servers have always stacked up (spooled) simultaneous print requests from many users, and then slowly printed (despooled) the jobs one at a time on a central printer. LANs would do this on the file server as a matter of course, but most networks required extra software to allow any workstation to also be a print server. Tucson, Arizona-based Artisoft set a new standard in 1987 when its LANtastic let any workstation print on any other user's printer.

Over the years print server software has gone beyond printing multiple documents on a first-come first-serve basis. Now many LANs allow users to rush a special print job past others for immediate printing.

Performance Technology's PowerLAN software will "shop" a print job among all the printers on the network, looking for the first printer available that can handle the job. Consider PowerLAN if you want to gang together 5 $600 Okidata laser printers to give you an unheard-of total print speed of 30 pages per minute, for example.

The 90s has seen the proliferation of new kinds of servers. Data communications and fax servers share high-speed modems and precious phone lines in one part of a building among everyone on the network. Database servers accept complex search requests from users and get back to them with the answers. In contrast, a file server doesn't search anything—it just pushes entire files back to the user that the user then has to sift through.

A LAN's appearance changes from different points of view as well as from different historical perspectives. Originally users saw LANs as a way of sharing exotic hardware among familiar desktop computers. Now, some managers see LANs as a centralized message facility, recording what everyone in an organization is doing. Computer consultants and designers see them as customizable replacements for mainframe dinosaurs. Computer companies see them as the next sales frontier—only a small percentage of potential LAN users have made a purchase yet. Whatever your point of view, if you handle information in your work, you will want to know about LANs.

The Journey Begins

The ancient Chinese had a well-known saying: "A picture is worth a thousand words." That is why we've included illustrations in this book. We want you to have a complete map to help you navigate your way around a LAN.

The ancient Chinese also had a saying, "A journey of a thousand miles begins with but a single step." Your first step is to take a few minutes and walk through Chapter 1. You might be amazed at just how quickly you can learn.

Chapter 1

Getting to Know Your LAN

A *network* is a group of independent computers in continuous communication with each other. A *Local Area Network* (LAN) is a group of computers connected in such close communication that they appear to their operators as individual entry points to a single repository of programs and information. In many ways, this could be thought of as having separate doorways to a single room.

This chapter will explain why you should consider using a LAN, and introduce you to the basic parts. Understanding LANs starts with a clear idea of what individual users do with their computers. If you are not familiar with personal computers (PCs), please read *Welcome to Personal Computers*, by Kris Jamsa, also available from MIS:Press.

9

How a Network Can Save You Money

Consider how you might benefit in the following areas:

▼ Efficiency

Sharing information among individuals can save large blocks of time if implemented properly. In many cases, LANs can eliminate redundancies, such as when two or more individuals, all of them working on the same project, each duplicate the work of the others because none of them knows exactly what part of the project each of the others is working on. LANs also make it possible to share expensive equipment, like laser printers and fax machines. And that also contributes to efficiency since people no longer have to waste time waiting in line to use those expensive machines.

Electronic Mail (E-mail)

Electronic mail is a very important way of increasing efficiency because it enables you to reach simple decisions and disseminate information without having meetings. E-mail can help executives make timely decisions by providing them with information quickly. If the person running an organization is hooked into the network with E-mail and other applications-sharing software, it's easier to keep abreast of what is happening over a large area. Figure 1.1 illustrates this idea.

Frontline personnel also benefit from having information more readily available. Customer service representatives, for example, are better able to answer customer questions. Without a network, information can be isolated in systems where customer representatives cannot get to it. In these cases, service personnel must write down the information requested, find an answer and call, then call back. Think about how much time and money would be saved if the representative had the information necessary to handle problems immediately; your customers couldn't help but be impressed.

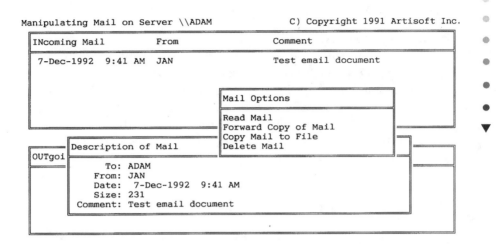

Figure 1.1 *A typical E-mail application will show the names of both sender and recipient, the time the message was sent, the size of the file, and will have space for a short comment. Your options generally include things like reading the mail, copying it to another file, forwarding it to another recipient, and deleting the message.*

N O T E Electronic mail can also help solve problems due to shift changes and travel schedules. For example, traveling sales reps can E-mail messages via a modem from their hotel rooms using a portable computer. A night shift worker can leave questions for the day shift worker that won't get lost in an in or out basket.

EASE OF DOCUMENTATION

Documentation is a good way of preventing costly communications errors. The harsh reality is that a lapse in communication caused by verbal communications can result in a misunderstanding, and something radically different from what you expected when you gave someone verbal instructions. How many times have you heard, "But I thought you meant . . ." Electronically transmitted records, such as E-mail, provide documentation that is especially helpful for projects involving many people and complex details over a long period of time. The ultimate goal for many companies is to create a paperless office. Having wide access to data files is a step in that direction.

REDUCED TRANSFER COSTS

Organizations that use standalone PCs tend to spend a good deal of time copying information from one hard disk or floppy disk to another. Jokingly referred to as *sneaker net*, this process involves physically carrying disks or mailing them from one location to another. A network, on the other hand, can allow fast transfer of information among machines within a network. Time savings increase significantly when your local network is connected to other networks within your organization regardless of their geographical location.

Standardization

These days there is much talk about *enterprise computing*; the computerization and interconnection of office and field workers throughout an organization. The goal of enterprise computing and, indeed, all networking, is to continuously share helpful information to the greatest extent practical. A properly implemented enterprise network gives a diversity of systems and software access to the same storage area. But to do this, some common method of communication between diverse systems must be chosen. This common method of communication is where standardization is essential. Such national technical bodies as the Institute for Electrical and Electronic Engineers (IEEE) spend a majority of their time researching and publishing equipment specifications. When implemented in products from the computer industry, standards are implemented to ensure that, for example, a computer from company A will be able to communicate with a computer from company B over a LAN produced by company C. Standards, however, are almost always voluntary. Except for regulating such things as potentially dangerous electromagnetic emissions there is no requirement beyond competitive pressure for any given manufacturer to produce "standard" hardware, software, and communications equipment.

Many network engineers have a drawer full of spare LAN adapters, and need them all. Every networking product has its own list of compatible boards.

Equipment Savings

In many cases, you can justify an investment in a network solely on the basis of equipment savings. You probably will end up buying fewer printers and other peripherals when you start using a network. You can also realize substantial savings on software by purchasing network versions. Multi-user versions of leading software packages are usually priced considerably less than it would cost to buy many single-user copies of the same program. This means that you can buy a program for 10, 20, or 30 workstations on a network for slightly more than it would cost to buy software for a couple of stand-alone PCs.

NOTE Many companies save additional money by phasing in their networks, especially when they are unsure of their long-term needs. Sometimes they start with a low-cost network, which can end up a throw-away or hand-me-down item to another department. In other words, you don't have to spend your entire management information systems (MIS) budget on networks at the beginning.

Downsizing

A final way in which a network can save you money is if you are in the process of "downsizing." An increasing number of organizations are finding that as personal computers continue their rapid growth in speed and power, the traditional role of the mainframe and minicomputer has been made redundant. As a result, a growing number of companies are using LANs and cheap, powerful PCs as complete replacements for their mainframes.

Downsizing is a more complex process than you might expect. Data processing and networking projects are notorious for overshooting budgets and time restrictions. Projects often take three times longer or more to complete than the original estimate.

DOWNSIZING PLANNING

Careful planning is essential if you hope to avoid many of the problems associated with downsizing from a mainframe to a LAN. Some of the major conversion issues include:

- **Finding PC equivalents to mainframe software.** Fortunately, PCs usually have software that does even more than mainframe software.

- **File conversion.** You will need to coordinate conversion of mainframe file formats to the formats required by your new software.

- **Testing.** You may want to run a pilot project first to iron out potential problems.

- **Transition Management.** Your backup and security programs will be starting from scratch. You will also need to ensure that your existing systems are operating during the transition. Don't forget to look at wiring and other equipment and facilities management issues.

- **Personnel.** You should have formal plans for training users. All user groups should be kept apprised of new procedures.

The Advantages and Disadvantages of LANs

LANs let you:

- Share expensive hardware and software with anyone on the network

- Reduce the chance of losing your data by broadcasting copies of important documents to several locations supporting centralized backup

- Reduce the chance of computer viruses and unauthorized data copying by having employees access shared data through "diskless workstations," that is, computer-like network terminals that have all of the capabilities of a regular PC and/or network workstation, except the ability to copy files onto a floppy disk

- Establish data and mail links between otherwise incompatible computer systems

- Arrange instant memo- and data-sharing between coworkers on group projects

- Soften the blow of individual computer crashes by letting you finish the crashed job immediately at some other workstation

However, LANs also make a few demands of their own:

- Someone will have to configure the LAN to ensure that a user's private data is not accidentally accessed by another user, or "published"

- Running wires between all the computers on a network can be expensive and time-consuming all by itself

- LANs can result in more dependency on outside consultants to plan and troubleshoot the system

A LAN does not make each computer connected to it more reliable. In fact, networked computers can be more finicky than "stand-alones." But taken as a whole, a well-designed LAN can keep critical software running 100% of the time. This is due to the LAN's ability to spread the work around in case of individual equipment failures.

When set up properly, a LAN is a solution to a specific kind of problem. The problem can be best expressed as "How can people who are already working together and using desktop computers increase their efficiency?" The solution is a computer-based system that allows easy communication and collaboration among all relevant users. This system most frequently will be a LAN.

Range

A LAN can span a single office or workgroup, a few floors in a building, or a few buildings. And while some types of LANs support hundreds of users, a typical LAN application will call for the network to support fewer than five people. The ability of a LAN to grow as your needs grow is called *expandability*, and is one of the hallmarks of all LANs. Most LANs can be changed or expanded easily, although just *how* easily depends as much on the design of the cabling plan as on the features of the particular LAN hardware and software. Growth usually happens either by adding new users to your developing LAN or by linking together smaller LANs. Creating a very large network from scratch is possible, but not all that common, and is sufficiently complex to be beyond the scope of what this book is all about—an introduction to the basic ins and outs of local area networking.

Reliability

LANs are known for reliability even when demand for network services is heavy. There are several reasons for the reliability of LANs. First, LAN system software typically includes features to detect, protect against, and correct transmission errors. Second, any LAN can have duplicate servers, that is, computers relied upon by others for their storage or printing ability. A second server, for example, may store backup copies of all files on the first server and can be activated instantly if the first server fails. This backup capability allows users to continue working while the first server is being repaired and reactivated.

Security

Since LANs help users share their data, they have an obligation to help users limit those with whom they want to share it. The choice by the LAN administrator of just who gets to access shared directories is the first barrier to unwanted intruders on the LAN. At this administrative level, only the people you choose as members of your workgroup will even see the directories you want them to access and have asked the LAN administrator to protect. When non-workgroup members sign on to the LAN, the protected directories don't even appear on their screens. The second level of intrusion protection is a system of passwords. User passwords are the best-known security feature. Most LANs not only require them to "get on the LAN," they can limit the time of day the passwords are valid and automatically "expire" old ones. Hardware data encryption in high-security installations scramble the data before broadcasting it. Rare until recently, data encryption has become more popular as LAN users start to communicate by public radio and cable links instead of private wires.

A New Way of Thinking

Stepping into the world of LANs requires a new way of looking at computers and how you use them. This requires a whole new vocabulary. LANs consists of:

- LAN Hardware
- LAN Software
- Nodes

LAN Hardware

LAN hardware consists of computers, including personal computers with special cards to promote linking, and such familiar devices as printers and modems. Personal computers come in two forms—clients and servers. *Clients* are personal computers that use services, files and applications made available by the network operating system. For example, a typical client would be a desktop computer requesting Lotus 1-2-3 from a NetWare file server. *Servers* are computers on a network enabling other files to share resources. A file server makes files and applications available to client computers. A print server enables client computers to share printing services across a network.

SERVERS

A server on a LAN is a computer accessed by multiple users for the purpose of running software or providing access to resources. A server can be a mainframe, minicomputer, or a personal computer. A workstation on the LAN connects to the server to run software.

Hubs

A *hub* is a device providing a central connection point for terminals, computers, or communications devices. LAN hubs range from simple write-management facilities to various switching devices and can serve a variety of purposes. In a typical application, the hub collects the data coming from several workstations and feeds it onto the main LAN cable (or trunk) for eventual delivery to the server.

Data Switches

A *data switch* is a device linking terminals, computers and other computer devices to a host computer. They are basically *concentrator devices*. A data switch has between 8 and 64 ports. Each data switch has a built-in microprocessor.

Network Management Stations

Many networks have special controlling devices that track packet transmissions as well as monitoring connections and error conditions. *Network management stations* (NMSs) gather information about these processes and store them on disks. That way, special problems can be detected.

LAN Software

LANs require special software to get computers to talk to each other. A network shell is loaded in the personal computer's memory and controls the communication of that personal computer with the network. This is also a centralized, server-based software component known as a network operating system (NOS). The NOS is the "traffic cop" that directs the operations of moving data around the LAN. Novell makes the most popular network operating system, Netware. However, other systems such as Artisoft's LANtastic are also very popular. Once the network is up and running, there are additional programs that are particularly suited to the work environment created by a LAN.

Group Scheduling

LANs are perfect for office workers struggling to arrange meetings and free time. With the high premium on everyone's time, computers and LANs have combined to ease the task of picking a mutually convenient spot on everyone's' calendar for holding essential face-to-face gatherings. Products such as Lotus Organizer and Chronologic's Instant Recall, Novell Groupwise, and Microsoft Schedule + are some of hundreds of appointment-tracking and daily reminder databases for personal computer networks. The key advantages of LAN schedulers over manual systems are:

- As soon as someone makes a change in a schedule, everyone affected by that change can be notified immediately.

- Computerized schedules can be searched in many more ways than paper ones. It's easy to ask:

  - After next Wednesday, when do I first have 3 hours free?

  - When will my partner and I have an hour free at the same time?

  - How many times have we met with someone from Company X in the last year?

They can even go out and find free time on everyone's schedule to set up the meetings.

GROUP PRODUCTIVITY

Other network software, such as Lotus Notes and other groupware productivity programs, stress the ability of individuals to work jointly on complex projects no matter where they are. They help users access, track, share, and organize information important to joint projects. Some even include pre-built templates for such activities as project management, account management, systems management, customer service, and so on. Such templates make it relatively easy for new users to quickly organize pertinent details in a way that is easy for others to understand—and being on the LAN makes this information easily accessible to other members of the workgroup.

FOREGROUND AND BACKGROUND

LANs are a common example of computers running more than one program at a time. For example, users can type text into their word processors while their last print job slowly dribbles out to a printer "in the background." But no matter how many programs are running, the user only pays attention to one program at a time.

The program that is catching the keystrokes from the user is said to be the *foreground program*. All other programs are considered to be running in background mode. Programs to receive faxes or send files while the user works at something else are examples of background programs and, while many people recognize the value of this type of program, you must always be aware that background programs unavoidably slow down the foreground program to some extent.

Nodes

Any device that is connected to a network is also called a *node*. Nodes include:

- personal computers
- communications devices
- printers
- servers

Each node will have an unique address. Its address is what identifies it to every other device on the LAN.

Packets

LANs transmit data in packets. You are already familiar with the idea of packets in every-day life. These are the little wrapped bundles delivered by United Parcel Service and other companies. In the world of LANs and electronic communication, a packet contains data exchanged between devices via a communication link. A LAN packet includes both the box and the contents of the box. Packets include:

- The address of the node sending the packet
- The address of the node receiving the packet
- The data to be transmitted
- Error control information

A typical packet holds 512 bytes of information. It takes many packets to transfer a large file over a network. The transmission rate in a LAN measures the rate at which bits travel across it. Transmission is usually measured in bits per second (bps).

PCs and Workstations

The most prominent physical components of a LAN fit on an individual desk. These components vary widely in their speed and features.

PERSONAL COMPUTERS

Most LANs are built around PCs or workstations that are powerful computers in their own right. They usually have the ability to store information permanently on magnetic internal hard disks or removable floppy disks. The exception, of course, would be inexpensive "diskless workstations."

Computers would be uselessly slow—if their only storage capability was in the form of mechanical disks spinning at the rate of 6 revolutions per second. "Loading" a program (temporarily storing it in random access memory) speeds thing up considerably. RAM computer chips store and retrieve information millions of times per second, making computers the useful tools that they are. A variant of storing information in system RAM is called *disk caching*. The term *cache* refers to a set of auxiliary RAM chips that are directly attached to the hard disk controller card. This cache is a temporary storage area for frequently-used data and, since information doesn't have to be sent to or retrieved from the physical hard disk, is a much faster way of accessing information. But RAM (whether system RAM or the RAM on a caching controller) needs constant electric power to operate, so it can not be relied on for permanent storage. Hence, users must pause for a few seconds and "save" a copy of the information they have processed from RAM onto their magnetic disks in case of a power outage or an equipment failure. Save your work at frequent intervals. Losing an hour's worth of work can be more than just an aggravation if it happens five minutes before a deadline!

After finishing this book we hope our readers will buy a $150 battery backup unit that will carry a computer through a few minutes of power failure.

The two most popular PC designs in today's offices are IBM-compatibles and Apple Macintoshes, as illustrated in Figure 1.2.

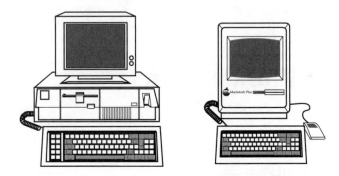

Figure 1.2 *Two most popular types of personal computers.*

IBM PCs

The IBM PC family, which originated in 1981, is the corporate standard throughout the United States. These days, however, IBM does not manufacture all members of this family. Typically, the very fastest IBM-type computers at any given time have been manufactured by someone else. IBM-compatible systems are built with components designed to comply with standards created and made available to other manufacturers by IBM, without violating IBM's patents or other laws. In general, IBM-compatible systems often are less expensive than equivalent systems manufactured by IBM. Some clones are sometimes built with components of less consistent quality than those of IBM-chosen parts. Many clones, however, are rated as highly as their IBM counterparts—if not higher. Zeos, Gateway, Dell and Compaq Computer Corporation, for example, manufacture IBM-compatible systems that are easily comparable to, and sometimes equipped with more features than, similar systems from IBM. Clones with such features are high-quality products, so many of the companies manufacturing them have been able to compete successfully with IBM. Today, pure IBM LANs are more rare than LANs that use at least one clone.

Macintosh

The second most popular family of desktop computer is the Macintosh, produced by Apple Computer Company Inc. Two Macintosh computers are pictured in Figure 1.3. The Mac, with its picture-oriented screens and emphasis on simplicity, attracted many adherents, even among corporate computing managers. Soon developers of leading business software from the IBM-compatible world began supplying Macintosh versions of their products.

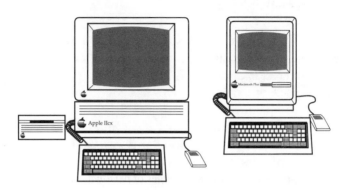

Figure 1.3 *Apple Macintosh computers.*

Today's crop of Macintosh computers comes equipped with sufficient power and memory to run animation and desktop publishing programs and, perhaps more to the point, with many networking capabilities built in. In addition, Macintosh computers now come with software that lets them read documents stored on the 3.5-inch floppy disks used by most 1990s IBM compatibles so that files in many formats can be quickly interchanged from one type of machine to the other. Many software manufacturers are also making dual platform software that works for both Macs and IBM-compatibles.

Workstations

Diskless workstations are desktop systems that cannot be used without a network connection. They have no ability to store data or programs from session to session. They typically only have high-speed RAM in which to run programs, and RAM, of course, is erased at each power-off. Diskless workstations are generally configured to turn on and immediately hook up to a network in order to find their programs and data.

NOTE

Any computer can be turned into a diskless workstation by removing its disk drives and installing the type of network interface card that will direct the computer to look for the network upon power-on.

Once hooked into the file storage services of the LAN, the diskless workstation is a perfectly functional computer, though always slower at loading large programs than it would be if it had its own disk drives.

While diskless workstations enjoyed something of a heyday in the mid- to late 80s, their popularity has suffered a decline in recent years. One reason for the fall-off in interest is that there is less economic incentive for a diskless workstation. The price of hard disk drives has continually fallen and is now so low that most companies find the economics of a diskless configuration less compelling. A second, and perhaps more interesting, reason for the workstation's decline is the surge in popularity of Windows. As the graphical user interface continues to win converts to the ease of point-and-click computing, more and more people find it difficult to operate a computer any other way. Windows' hook is that many Windows applications require a local hard disk. Thus, the scenario runs like this: for individuals to be productive, they need Windows software. For Windows software to operate at all, it needs a local hard disk. Since it's cheaper to buy a hard disk and keep people productive than it is to convert to non-Windows software and retrain the workforce, the diskless workstation has been virtually eclipsed.

Since you can turn a PC into a diskless workstation, it is usually possible to turn a diskless workstation back into a full PC! Computer upgrade shops will be glad to add the necessary disk drives. The price will depend on what your local shop charges for labor, plus the cost of the hardware. And hardware costs are continuing to decline. In most cases, the total price will be quite reasonable unless you decide to go for a truly huge hard drive.

NETWORK INTERFACE ADAPTERS

The heart of a personal computer is the *microprocessor*, which is wired to take its instructions from the computer's RAM chips. The microprocessor talks to RAM memory at the rate of at least 16 million characters of information (about a phone-book's worth) per second, and often 2 or 3 times faster than that! But LANs available today can only carry information at a fraction of that speed. Hence the need for special add-on boards or adapters, called *network interface card*s (NICs). These adapters also go by such names as LAN cards or network cards. The NIC collects information from the busy microprocessor, stores it, and doles it out slowly onto the network wires. Figure 1.4 shows typical network cards.

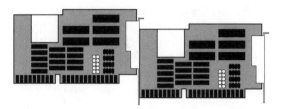

Figure 1.4 *Network interface cards.*

Consider also that microprocessors, like the one magnified in Figure 1.5, are tiny chips with no place to plug network wiring into them. So the right NIC for a LAN must also provide the style of physical connector that the network wires will be looking for.

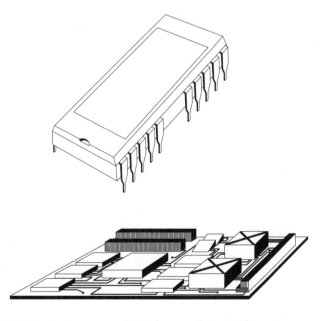

Figure 1.5 *A microprocessor chip. The one illustrated here gives you an idea what a typical ROM (read-only memory) chip looks like, but many types of RAM (random access memory) chips have a similar configuration.*

By the late 1990s most computers may come with popular NIC hardware as standard equipment. Indeed, most Apple Macintoshes already have Ethernet (a type of networking hardware) built into every box. But for now most of us will have to shop for NICs.

NICs can be characterized as "smart" and "dumb." The "dumb" NICs are simple, inexpensive, and use part of the host PC's processor power to help perform their job. "Dumb" NICs work fine in fast 386 and 486 machines (most new computers). "Smart" NICs have their own microprocessors and can be a good choice for older, slower computers or bigger, high-demand networks.

Network interface adapters vary in cost, usually beginning below $100. The price depends on the adapter's features and manufacturer. It will also be influenced by where you buy it—a retailer, discounter, or mail order operation. In recent years, several companies, such as Novell and 3Com, began lowering prices on network interface adapters.

Macintosh computers, unlike most IBM-compatible PCs, come already equipped to participate in networks based on AppleTalk, which is Apple Computer's own network. Instead of extra network cards, most Macintosh computers are connected to a network via their printer ports, which double as what Apple calls *LocalTalk connectors*. Unfortunately, this Apple-designed network is slow and somewhat limited. Fortunately, most Macintosh computers can be equipped with a network interface adapter like an IBM-compatible PC.

Adapters that plug into the Macintosh disk drive port are available also, as are devices that act as bridges from Macintosh-based networks to networks designed primarily for IBM PCs and compatibles.

TIP   Token Ring and Ethernet adapters have unique addresses assigned at the factories. They are six bytes, half assigned to describe the board's manufacturer and half representing the board as assigned by the factory. ARCnet networks have user definable addresses. ARCnet is a LAN type that features a physical bus and a logical star.

MODEMS

To form a LAN, a desktop system and its components must have some sort of physical access to the wire over which network messages are transmitted. As we saw in the previous section, most IBM-compatible PCs and many Macintoshes use network interface cards. Network interface cards share many features with a broader type of communications device called a *modem*. The modem performs the same tasks via a telephone line that a network interface adapter does in a LAN, allowing the PC user the ability to communicate with other users and other computers. What makes a modem particularly relevant to a LAN-user is the fact that, given the right kind of software, remote PCs can "dial in" to a LAN, allowing users literally anywhere in the world access to programs and information stored on the LAN. Modems can also be used to connect your LAN to the Internet. Most commonly, modems on a network are attached to a device called a *communications server*.

One of the most popular early modems was manufactured by Hayes Microcomputer Products. Today, Hayes compatibility has become the de facto standard for modems.

While many modems come with their own proprietary software, you can also order special communications programs. Cross Talk and ProComm are two of the most popular.

TIP

Logging On

Many, if not most personal computer users, can start most programs with great ease, usually a matter of just clicking on an icon or typing a word. Working with network software requires a login script for setting up the environment to network users. This script is a series of commands that execute when a user logs in. The commands placed in log in scripts:

- map network drives for uses
- switch users to specific drives
- display menus
- start applications

In most network environments, there is one login script attached to the login account for each user. This script will run when a user logs in. In some cases, however, logging in is as simple as clicking on an icon.

SERVERS AND PRINTERS

Most PC users are already familiar with hard disk drives—the magnetic storage devices where they keep most of their files and the programs they use for applications such as word processors, spreadsheets, or databases. Even after expanding into a LAN most users continue to keep copies of their own files on that hard drive. But if you need to share your data with others, or you would like some administrator to make safety copies of your files for you, storage of your data over the LAN into a central file server can make your life a lot easier.

As mentioned earlier, a *server* is any LAN computer that will service requests from others for information or action. Most LANs are set up with at least one file server that anyone on the LAN can command to store or retrieve information for them. The beauty of a LAN is that this remote, central storage takes place with no extra effort by the user. The file server appears to users as just another disk drive that seems to be everywhere at all times.

Similarly, a computer with an expensive printer hooked up to it can be set up as a print server, taking print jobs from all corners. Figure 1.6 illustrates this concept.

With peer-to-peer networks (discussed later in this chapter) any computer can be a server. Even a diskless workstation could be a print server. Peer-to-peer users can at any time decide if they will share any (or all) of their computer's powers with other people on the LAN.

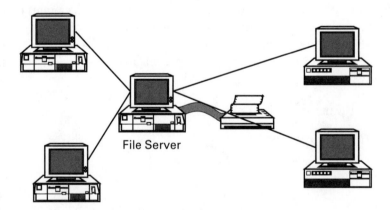

File Server

Figure 1.6 *A file and print server.*

DEDICATED VERSUS NON-DEDICATED SERVERS

Many networks will let their users run standard programs while their computers are simultaneously functioning as network servers. A computer that both runs standard programs and lets other users see its data at the same time is said to be a *non-dedicated server*. Non-dedicated servers can be a clever way of setting up a LAN without having to buy any extra computers. When they join the LAN the non-dedicated servers are just commanded to do more things at once.

The problem with a non-dedicated server, though, is the human operator! Should the operator do something to the server to make it crash, every user on the LAN relying on that server may lose the data they are working on. So high-reliability/high-speed LANs set aside a whole computer to service the LAN.

A computer without a human operator, whose only job is to harbor shared data and process a user's requests for access to printers, is called a *dedicated server*. To increase reliability, some LAN managers even disconnect the keyboards from dedicated servers so that no one can disrupt the servers' work.

Dedicated servers are faster than non-dedicated, since they don't have to run programs for anyone. They concentrate on broadcasting data and taking print requests as quickly as possible. So dedicated server computers don't have to be as fast as their non-dedicated counterparts.

As a case in point, since the only thing dedicated servers do is share their disk drives, many small LANs work nicely with a slow 386. Additionally, the cost to your organization in lost productivity from just one server crash could easily be much greater than the cost of setting up a dedicated server in the first place. For all but the smallest LANs, consider investing in a dedicated server.

Increasingly, offices are setting up multiple servers. A second server, for example, can store backup copies of all data on the primary server. It can even be programmed to automatically take over should the primary server fail. Spare servers allow network users to continue working while the first server is being fixed. Some LANs have all their servers in one place for easy care and repair. Others purposely spread the servers throughout the office—there's less chance that a single catastrophe will make the dispersed servers all fail at once.

There is considerable choice in terms of network operating system software when you start looking at dedicated server-based networks. Chapter 6 details many of the most popular selections currently on the market.

Peer-to-Peer Networks

An exciting development for cost-conscious buyers has been the development of *peer-to-peer networks*. These networks are one step above zero-slot LANs, which are systems that simply connect several computers by tying their serial ports together, and one step below a dedicated-server network. These systems are frequently less expensive to install and maintain than are full networks, but do offer such traditional LAN features as file-transfer and printer-sharing capabilities.

On a technical basis, a peer-to-peer network is distinguished by its ability to have any networked computer also be a common file or print server for all other networked computers. Any computer on the network can be summarily drafted into serving all the other computers. No user has any more or less access to the network than any other, hence they are all "peers." Instead, any machine can be made to be a resource shared by all the others on the same network. The other machines on the network can access files on the hard disk of the conscripted computer and can use the printers and other peripherals attached to it.

As we shall see when we discuss LANtastic from Artisoft and Novell's NetWare Lite in Chapter 6, peer-to-peer systems have the advantage of being relatively simple, relatively cheap, and using very little memory—only 10 to 20K of memory on the workstations and as little as 40 to 50K on the station that also acts as the server.

The disadvantages of such a solution are similar to those of zero-slot LANs, namely:

- limited growth potential
- lack of connectivity to other vendors' networks

Another key disadvantage of the peer-to-peer LAN is that it provides less security than desired by secrecy-conscious firms. Yet, even the Internal Revenue Service and many banks have felt comfortable using such LANs. For a small company without major plans for expansion, or for a home office where secrecy is not likely to be an issue, this type of solution can be an excellent alternative to dedicated-server networks.

WINDOWS FOR WORKGROUPS

Microsoft Windows for Workgroups is the peer-to-peer version of Windows, the popular operating environment made by Microsoft. With Windows for Workgroups, any 386 or later model system can act as a server. Any personal computer can work as a client. You can also use Workgroup Connection for MS-DOS to connect an MS-DOS-based PC as a client to a Windows for Workgroups server. Windows for Workgroups is renowned for its simple installation. You can buy Windows for Workgroups starter kits containing software, network cards and cables; hardware and software kits; or software-only kits, depending on what you need.

Windows for Workgroups is compatible with Novell Netware IBM's OS/2 LAN Server and Windows NT. Organizations who already have networks can use Windows for Workgroups as a client to bring new capacities to existing LAN users, including workgroup-enabled applications, scheduling and Network Dynamic Data Exchange (NDDE). It features Microsoft Mail, an electronic mail service, and opens the door to common workgroup activities, such as document assembly, schedule tracking, information sharing, and forms routing and notification. Windows for Workgroups contains Schedule+, a full-featured graphical scheduling application that allows you to manage a daily calendar and task lists. It also helps you schedule group meetings by letting you view other users' schedules, so you can find mutually agreeable times to get together.

N O T E Network DDE lets users create compound documents that share data across a network. You can insert information in your documents from those owned by other users on other computers. Network DDE ensures that changes made to an original document will be made to all supporting documents across a network.

N O T E

Let's say, for example, you are the head of a workgroup working on an annual report and you included graphics from the art department, text from the marketing department and financial data from the marketing department. Any time the marketeer, the artist, or the accountant makes a change in their supporting documents, the change can automatically be made in our annual report file.

Windows For Workgroups Security

Security features in Windows for Workgroups allow users to restrict access to directories on two levels, Read-Only and Full Access. With Read-Only directories users can view files in a shared directory, but cannot change or delete files. With Full-Access rights, users can change existing files, add new files, and delete files.

Windows NT

A server and workstation network that works in almost the same way as Windows for Workgroups is called *Windows NT*. Meant to compete with the powerful but often complex operating system known as UNIX, this is the newest generation of Windows. It is a 32-bit operating system which works on several processors, including Intel's 386, 486 and Pentium, DEC Alpha-based 64-bit Reduced Instruction Set Computers RISC and MIPS R4000 64-bit RISC, as well as "super server" systems that use a combination of processors and special designs. Windows NT's ability to fully access 32-bit processors allows it to work with larger numbers, memory addresses, and instructions. This means that overall throughput, the combination of processor performance, data transfer, and memory access (in other words, speed), will improve.

The Windows NT user interface looks pretty much like the Windows 3.1 interface. It runs thousands of Windows 3.1 and MS-DOS applications. It also supports OS/2 applications. Like any other version of Windows, Windows NT programs are arranged in groups. You double-click the icon of the program you want to activate it.

Windows NT also includes built-in networking and advanced security features. The target market includes end users who need performance and the ability to switch among multiple applications, and workgroup users who need to share their system with other users. Windows NT is also technically very efficient—it encourages multitasking. *Multitasking* means that operating systems can do several things at once. With Windows NT's multitasking capability, if one task gets held up accessing a slow device such as a disk, the process can turn its attention to other tasks. The program also includes several memory protection capacities.

Putting It All Together

A network consists of two or more computers that are connected to each other. Networks are designed to enable computers to share resources, such as printers, as well as to exchange information and share files. Some networks have central servers. Users working on a network must log into the file server, which performs many of the central management functions of the network. Other networks use a peer-to-peer system, which is less expensive and uses a "superstation" workstation with extra memory instead of a central server. Each machine on a peer-to-peer network can be a resource shared by others on that network.

A LAN is a network restricted to a specific area of a building and connected by high-speed cabling.

Glossary

ARCnet

A LAN that features a physical bus and logical star. ARCnet networks have user definable addresses.

background

A task that is running on a workstation independent of user attention and is simultaneous to foreground work.

client

A personal computer that uses services, files, and applications made available by the file server.

communications server

Most commonly, modems on a network are attached to a device called a communications server. A server is any LAN computer that will service requests from others for information or action; in this case, connection (via modems) to an outside network.

concentrator device   A device linking terminals and computers to a host.

data switch   A device linking terminals, computers, and other computer devices to a host computer. They are basically concentrator devices. A data switch has between eight and 64 ports. Each data switch has a built in microprocessor.

dedicated server   A computer without a user, set aside to run network software, providing highest-performance network-wide data storage and printing services.

disk caching   A set of auxiliary RAM chips that are directly attached to the hard disk controller card. This cache is a temporary storage area for frequently used data, and, since information doesn't have to be sent to or retrieved from the physical hard disk, is a much faster way of accessing information.

disk server   A hard disk used to share files with several users; the precursor of the file server.

DOS   Abbreviation for *Disk Operating System*. DOS is the most commonly used operating system in PCs.

E-mail   A system to send messages among users of a computer network, or the software that supports these message transfers.

enterprise computing   The computerization and interconnection of office and field workers throughout an organization.

file server   A centralized storage device complete with software that can be accessed by several users of a network.

foreground   A task running on a workstation that is the focus of user attention.

hard disk	A data recording medium built into a PC.
hub	A device providing a central connection point for the connecting of terminals, computers, or communication devices. LAN hubs range from simple write-management facilities to various switching devices and can serve a variety of purposes.
LAN	Abbreviation for *local area network*. A typical LAN will consists of peripheral devices and computers contained in the same building, often on the same floor.
microprocessor	The heart of a personal computer, the microprocessor is a silicon chip which is wired to take its instructions from the computer's RAM chips.
modem	A device that takes data from a computer and translates it into a form that can travel over a telephone line or that takes electronic signals traveling via telephone and makes them usable by a computer.
multitasking	The ability to do several things at once.
network interface card	A circuit board allowing a direct connection from a personal computer to a network cable.
network operating system	Special software to get computers to talk to each other.
nondedicated server	A server that can also be used as a workstation.
operating system	Software program that your computer runs when it first starts.
peer-to-peer network	A network that uses a "superstation" workstation with extra memory instead of a central server.
personal computer	A microcomputer, also known as a *PC*.
Private Branch Exchange (PBX)	Sophisticated and heavily centralized telephone system.

RAM   Abbreviation for *Random Access Memory*, the computer's electronic memory.

ROM   Abbreviation for *Read Only Memory*, the computer's pre-programmed memory.

server   On a network, a special computer giving users access to services such as file sharing or resource sharing.

sneaker net   Copying information from one hard disk or floppy disk to another. This process involves physically carrying disks (presumably while wearing sneakers) from one location to another.

terminal   A desktop device that usually includes a screen and keyboard like a workstation or PC, but is incapable of performing operations unless it is connected to a computer.

topology   The physical layout of devices on a network.

workstation   A PC that grants a user access to a network. Some workstations have disk drives, others do not.

zero slot LAN   A LAN that does not require a network interface card.

Chapter 2

Assessing Your Network Needs

It is not unusual for unsuspecting people to suddenly find themselves appointed head of the newly created "bureau of LAN management." Perhaps you are one of these people. In many cases, this person has the more official title "LAN administrator." Either way, these people are likely to feel like they've been dropped into a cauldron of hot confusion, waiting to sink or swim.

Many turn to LAN consultants for help. While this strategy can be effective, remember that, at best, consultants help sporadically and are not at the work site every day. At worst, because there is no formal certification procedure for consultants, they may be incompetent. The more you know about LANs, however, the more likely you are to make wise decisions, including selecting a competent consultant.

The best remedy for hysteria is to plan before you LAN. This chapter will tell you how. After you have assessed your needs, you can decide which computers you want to connect, how you want to wire them together, and what network operating system you want to use.

Recognizing What You Need

Many times managers will call in consultants to ask the question, "Which LAN should I get?" The problem is that they have already decided to purchase a LAN. A more logical question would be, "Should I get a LAN?"

A microcomputer manager needs to justify a decision to install or expand a LAN. The manager will need a plan to ensure that networked computing solutions will meet the needs of the users today and in the near future. Preparing a LAN proposal is a two-step process: *assessment* and *planning*.

Assessment

Before you buy clothes you try them on. Sometimes, if the clothing is custom tailored you will try it on several times and make alterations. Obviously you will want to take similar precautions when you start investigating LANs. The first step in buying clothing is to determine your size. Similarly, the first step in purchasing a LAN is to take some measurement, that is, perform a needs assessment. In other words, ask yourself, "How much LAN do I need?"

Another way of thinking about a needs assessment is as a road map. The process should tell you where you are and the possible routes that will take you to your destination. For an assessment to work, managers and workers have to cooperate. On one hand, workers know where the most important computers are located. They are also most likely to know what problems occur most often. There is no substitute for hands-on knowledge. On the other hand, managers need to record these observations and work toward finding solutions that fit. Workers point out the landmarks, managers draw the map.

Obviously, an assessment means more work for users and managers, at least in the short run. The temptation may be to just leave things the way they are. However, this extra work may be the key difference between finding a needed solution and facing an unavoidable problem. Most organizations are becoming increasingly dependent on their computing resources. As such dependence grows, so does the importance of having PCs and LANs that are easy to understand and reliable.

Your needs assessment should begin with a comprehensive examination of your existing structures: your physical office layout, your workflow, your PCs, and the programs people use independently. If you already have a network, you need to look at what kind you have, how it is laid out, and whether you can meet your needs by revising it or if you need to replace it with something entirely different.

The next question you should ask is, "What information and resources need sharing in my work group?" You will want to review the methods that are already used for sharing this information. Meanwhile, you need to ask whether these methods are adequate. As we shall see in later chapters, a LAN is not always the answer. Indeed, no one will tell you that every group of PC-using co-workers needs a LAN.

In some cases, you may not even need a high-tech solution. Let's say, for example, you're assessing the needs of an art department composed of five artists, all of whom have PCs. You only have a part-time receptionist to answer phone calls. The problem is that messages get lost when the receptionist isn't around. Possibly, a LAN with voice mail software would work best to get everyone their messages all the time. The problem, however, is that voice mail is impersonal. A better solution may be to hire the receptionist full-time or to use a live answering service. That way you won't sacrifice the "personal touch."

If you have the money, you may still want to use a LAN to forward those messages to the right parties. You should be aware, however, that this solution will require extra work and has hidden costs. Someone will need to:

- Select the right software
- Find the right hardware
- Authorize payment for it
- Get it installed and working
- Make sure it is maintained
- Ensure that everyone is trained to use it

Although you may already have a LAN in place, it may not be the best solution. Evaluate how your current system works before you make new purchases. This evaluation should be an ongoing process involving managers, vendors, and colleagues. Keep notes on ideas and questions as they occur. In many cases, the more you know, the more questions you will have.

Assessments, moreover, need to be reviewed and updated regularly, especially just before making a purchase decision. In the long run, good assessments help guarantee that equipment users and managers, as well as the entire organization, end up with plans for important decisions about available computing resources. In any event, a LAN solution should address both current and future needs. Many consultants recommend buying or expanding systems based on needs six months down the line.

The best needs assessments often begin with quantitative details such as the number of hours a day your group uses word processing software versus database programs. You may also want to count the number of people involved in each current project. Counting such things as the number of hours spent on particular tasks and the number of users involved in those tasks forms the basis for LAN selections. Repeat your survey later to measure the effects of ongoing incremental changes, such as the introduction of new hardware or software.

Eventually you will want to look at the projected impact of any proposed changes. For example, if you get a LAN, will you need new software? If so, will you and your coworkers need time off to learn how to use this new software?

WORKING WITH CONSULTANTS

As you can see, an assessment can be a long and involved process. That is why many organizations call on a consultant for help. The idea is to borrow the expertise of someone who has been through the process many times. Hiring a consultant, however, is an art form in its own right.

Consultants and contractors are hired for relatively short periods to work on specific projects. They are paid by the project, by the day, or by the hour. The term *consultant*, however, is very broad and includes many levels and types. Contractors, for example, generally work for themselves, independent of any umbrella consulting firm. They are generally directly paid on an hourly fee basis. Traditional consultants, on the other hand, are generally members of a consulting firm and are paid a salary by the firm while you pay the firm a fee based on a negotiated per-project, per-hour, or per-day rate. Obviously, the firm takes a markup to cover its overhead and make a profit.

Differences also exist in the focus of particular consultants. Some emphasize strategic planning and tend to be very expensive. Others are more willing to work at lower levels within the organization, providing training or diagnosis.

Different consultants use different approaches. There is no such thing as a standard one-size-fits-all policy. A manager considering soliciting a consultant's advice on your work group's computing solution should discuss the consultant's procedures and how they will affect workers. Will the consultant conduct the interviews? Will he or she insist that workers keep logs of their computer time?

As a safeguard, some management experts recommend that you insist up front that you be allowed to end your relationship with the consultant after the assessment is completed and delivered to you. Otherwise, the argument goes, a consultant may be overly motivated to recommend changes in his or her best interest but may not guarantee the best possible solution. However, you can avoid this dilemma by specifying that a contract is for diagnosis only.

Any time you hire a consultant, you need to ask:

- Has the consultant been in business long enough to have both breadth and depth in training, design, and delivery?

- What is this consultant's reputation among peers and clients? Ask for a list of references and make sure you contact them.

- Will the consultant's personality help the project? Indeed, most experts will tell you that good consulting is nine-tenths personal chemistry.

- Do you trust the consultant to make good decisions and deliver value and quality?

Planning

Planning is especially important with LANs because LANs are complex, and there are many things that can go wrong. Be prepared to tinker with your solution once you choose it. Planning, after all, is the art of making those adjustments. You will need to make plans for:

- choosing consultants
- selecting maintenance contractors
- choosing an installer
- training existing staff
- hiring new staff
- changing job descriptions
- security
- backups
- upgrades

The estimation of costs is part of planning. Equipment costs are only the tip of the iceberg. You also have to take into consideration added expenses, such as those brought about by using consultants or adding new personnel. In many cases, costs provide a make-or-break decision. The goal is to spend as little money as possible while getting the maximum benefit. In the real world, however, that means setting a reasonable price.

Basic budgeting usually involves some sort of cost/benefit analysis. You spend money not for the sake of spending money, but because you want to achieve something. Your analysis will tell you whether the costs justify the anticipated result.

Costs are easier to estimate than benefits. A specific project's costs can usually be broken down into such components as:

- Hardware
- Software
- Training

- Maintenance
- Supplies
- Personnel
- Installation

Larger organizations also take into consideration costs associated with such problems as downtime. When a system malfunctions, costs are incurred for lost labor, replacement of files (usually not a problem if there is sufficient backup), and other inconveniences. These calculations can become very complex. *Risk analysis*, as it is called, is an important part of the decision making process in large organizations. Smaller organizations often remain satisfied with calculating out-of-pocket expenses.

Benefits are usually harder to quantify, although sometimes you can estimate savings. Hard costs come from the elimination of line items. For example, if you buy the $500 version of network software for your 20-station network, you can save $5500 over buying 20 individual copies for stand-alone PCs.

Soft costs, which cover intangible benefits, tend to be more common, but also more difficult to pin down. In many cases, the soft benefits, if properly analyzed, outweigh tangible benefits. One key intangible benefit of getting or expanding a LAN is the ability to stay state-of-the-art by moving to the next level of sophistication. You can also make the argument that a LAN can provide a competitive advantage (by increasing customer service, for example). While it is hard to estimate the exact dollar amount attached to this kind of "image improvement," the fact remains that your customers judge you on what they perceive about you. They want to know that they are dealing with an organization that will be able to meet their needs in the future, as well as right now.

Budgeting techniques range from the very simple to the very complex. Many organizations, even small ones, set aside a certain amount of money for MIS solutions. Money goes for equipment and human resources. At its simplest level, individuals responsible for making the systems work do the best they can with what they have, adding resources as results are obtained. This is the most common procedure in small businesses.

Another common budgeting method, especially with smaller companies, is to plan expenditures as a percentage of total sales. A company will use industry averages as the basis for this percentage. This percentage can be low in the case of restaurants and dry cleaners; it can be high, as in insurance companies.

PAYBACK AND ROI

Larger organizations use budgeting techniques promoted by business schools. The two most common are *payback period* and *return on investment* (ROI). Payback period is easier to understand because the principle is based on the amount of time required to recover an initial investment.

For example, you invest $1000 in a LAN. To determine the payback period you would have to calculate just how long it would take to save that much money as a direct result of making the investment. In our example, if you saved $500 each year on software, the payback period would be two years. If, on the other hand, you saved only $200 each year, the payback period would be five years.

ROI budgeting is more complex. It involves a formula that uses the banking discount rate and, because the discount rate changes, the formula changes. The ROI formula tries to find out what the current value of all savings resulting from a purchase will be. In other words, how much will your future savings be worth in today's dollars?

For example, if you were given a chance to save $10 ten years from now or $5 today, which would you choose? You should pick the $5 today because it is worth more. (After all, do you remember how much more you could buy for the same amount ten years ago than you could buy today?) That's why under ROI budgeting a savings of $10,000 some years in the future could be worth $5000 or less today.

Information Systems Goals

Some consultants recommend that you start with an assessment of business goals and then come up with a mission-critical statement for your LAN. A mission-critical statement would come from organizational soul searching and would define those areas that are most essential to your organization's success. It would answer the following two questions:

1. What activities make the difference between success and failure in your company?

2. How do these activities relate to your current system?

You would want to give top priority to LANs that improve quality or output in these essential functions, but the definition of an "essential function" changes from organization to organization. For example, an automobile dealer would give a much higher priority to any procedure or equipment purchase that can increase sales or improve service. In a hospital, patient care would take precedence over such support functions as billings or supplies.

The first challenge for most work groups and smaller organizations, however, is less esoteric. Most organizations start with the fairly narrow focus of setting information system goals. The first step is to inventory what you already have. You need to ask yourself questions such as:

- What hardware do I have?

- What software do I have?

- What problems do I have with software and hardware?

- How much growth can my current system handle?

- What changes would I like to make?

Goals

Now you are ready to actually set goals. The easiest way to set goals is to look at your competitors and other organizations doing similar work and learn from them. The following questions are a good place to start:

- Do you know another organization trying to achieve the same goals? If so, what can you learn from them?

- What are your competitors doing to enhance their systems?

Goal setting is an art form in its own right. Most consultants recommend that you set quantifiable goals, such as increasing profits by 10 percent over a nine-month period or decreasing average billing time 12 percent within six months. However, beyond the obvious mathematics of goal setting, you also need to factor in the human element. Are the people you are working with committed to these goals? If you are committed to a goal, you are more likely to reach it.

Realistic Budget Assessment and Justification

The simplest way of coming up with a realistic budget is to ask yourself, "How much can I afford to spend?" Don't spend more than you can afford. You may want to consider making purchases in stages, so that you don't have to pay a lump sum. Also, you need to remember to include items such as maintenance and training in your budget. Estimating benefits, as mentioned earlier, is trickier than estimating costs; benefits tend to be intangible. The tools of financial analysis often overlook many of the true benefits of a new system, including:

- Increased morale
- Competitive advantage
- Increased customer satisfaction
- State-of-the-art technological positioning

Smaller organizations sometimes think they only need to consider budgets or benefits when they are in crisis. Companies that are run from this type of management-by-crisis mode usually make commitments in a reactionary manner, aimed at solving an immediate problem and nothing more. Wise companies, regardless of size, focus on solving problems before they reach the "meltdown" stage. If your organization does not have this proactive type of orientation, information systems planning may be a good place to start.

A Cautionary Reminder

Don't make the mistake of thinking that just because you have mastered the art of working with independent PCs, you are a LAN expert. Working with LANs is a more intricate process. Although your organization probably will not have to hire a full-time technician to handle your LAN, your new equipment will require special attention.

Many smaller companies end up having a part-time LAN manager or dividing the responsibilities among several people. For this strategy to work, your workforce has to be convinced that the commitment to learning a new system is justified. In most cases, of course, it will be.

However, smaller companies often have to choose between technologies that are important but not essential and services that are essential to growth or survival, such as salespersons' salaries or advertising budgets. No small company should invest in new technology for the sake of investing in technology. Fortunately, the newer generation of low-cost easy-to-use systems avoids most of these problems for both large and small companies.

There is also a temptation to become overly dependent on consultants. Try to avoid this. At some point (and the sooner the better), you have to shoulder the responsibility of learning to operate and maintain your own LAN. You'll save money, you'll learn something new, and you'll give yourself the ability to handle problems more quickly and efficiently. Even the best consultant cannot be at your fingertips all day.

Requests for Proposal

Once your organization has assessed its needs and made plans to make purchases, the next step is often to issue a *Request for Proposal* (RFP). Your organization makes this request available to vendors who then make bids. The art of RFPs can, and has, filled several books. However, for an idea of what a typical LAN RFP looks like, see Appendix C.

IBM Versus Clones

Which type of PC will you use? Even if you don't end up getting a LAN, sooner or later your organization will face this question. At one time, if you wanted the best computers, the answer was IBM. Even today, the term IBM PC is used interchangeably with personal computers (except Macintoshes).

These days, of course, there are numerous clone manufacturers who produce PCs. The important point of this increased competition is that, since the beginning of this decade, PC manufacturers have been waging a price war. The recession, periodic slumps in PC sales, and deep discounting by clone vendors have forced even IBM to slash prices to regain market share. Today, IBM faces competition from high-quality clones that sometimes have better support and service than IBMs.

The thing to remember when hardware shopping these days is that quality is often less a matter of label than of your local source of supply. With price being less of a factor, *support*, *service*, and the *overall number* of features you can include on a system should be major factors in your purchase decision. With its increased emphasis on customer friendliness and lower prices, the old adage that "nobody ever got fired for buying IBM" is still true. On the other hand, your local computer retail outlet is where you're going to go if you have problems, so check out as many local sources of supply as you can. Don't be too put off if you're not personally familiar with all the brands in all the stores. Pay more attention to whether the personnel behind the counter pay attention to you when you ask questions and whether they have a reputation for standing behind whatever brands they sell. It's also important to note that several manufacturers, such as Dell Computer and Zenith Data Systems, have specialized business-to-business sales efforts that cater to LAN customers. If a particular system's features catch your attention, it's easy—and potentially profitable—to investigate any discount deals that may be offered.

PCs Versus Macs

Macintosh computers carved their niche in the popular consciousness as "the computer for the rest of us" by capitalizing on the point-and-click user interface (see Figure 2.1) developed by Xerox at its Palo Alto Research Center.

Microsoft broadened the mouse-and-pointer approach to computing by developing Windows for the less-expensive PC-type computers that the majority of businesses and individuals owned. A typical screen is shown in Figure 2.2. IBM's recent emphasis on OS/2 (another point-and-click interface) widens our choices still further.

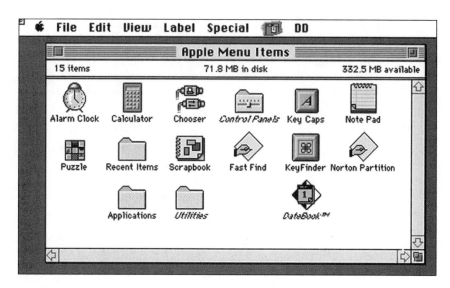

Figure 2.1 *Macintosh user interface, showing icons that represent individual applications.*

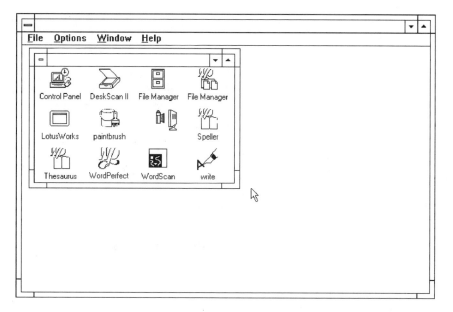

Figure 2.2 *A Windows screen. Here, too, icons represent applications you can run simply by pointing to the icon with the arrow on the screen and double-clicking a mouse button. The OS/2 user interface from IBM has a similar appearance.*

Today, with software vendors emphasizing programs that work the same on both Macs and PCs and whose files can be shared between users on both types of computers (called *"cross-platform" development*), the choice of which machine you want to use is often a matter of personal taste. Further, with IBM and Apple jointly backing the new RISC-based PowerPC, the old dividing lines between "us" and "them" have become even more obscured. The end result for us end users is that we now have unparalleled choice in the machines and programs we can effectively use—and the ability of our hardware and software to communicate with someone else's hardware and software grows on an almost daily basis. Practically any system you buy will emphasize the use of graphics to present information to users. We simply press a button on a mouse to:

- Move information around

- Launch (or start) applications

- Invoke commands

The nagging drawback that has continued to haunt the Macintosh is its sticker price. Although Macintosh computers have gained in popularity, many people object to their expense. However, Mac proponents counter that, especially with regard to LANs, base price is deceiving. For example, Macs have networking capabilities built right into the system hardware and software. Today many are preconfigured with powerful Ethernet interfaces. These are LAN-oriented considerations you have to take into account when you go computer shopping. Macs still cost more than PCs, but their features and the reduced amount of fooling around you have to do to get them running on a LAN may make you want to take a second look.

Ethernet Versus Token Rings

When networks were first developed for mainframes and minicomputers, they were fairly simple: One type of network software ran on one type of cabling between computers that had to be of the same type. For example, if you bought Digital Equipment Corporation (DEC) gear, you had to connect to DEC equipment to make it work.

Networks are much more complex today. Communicating between devices on the network is similar to people talking. You need a common way to send and receive messages so that they are understandable to both parties exchanging information. LANs, however, include some way for controlling access to the media shared by all the connected devices. Without these controls, LANs could not work. It would be like a postal system where everyone just threw their letters into mail boxes and hoped that somehow the right person would get their mail. Our postal system, however, requires the use of ZIP codes to steer the mail to specific areas containing even more specific addresses to shared communications facilities.

LAN operating systems manage access to their network media. In fact, many LAN operating systems support several different access methods. Some network access methods are *random*, which means they allow any connected device to request access to the shared medium at any time. Most office LANs depend on random access. Others are deterministic and use predefined rules and conditions to assign access priority to the various devices on a network.

Ethernet

Ethernet is the most popular method for connecting devices and is used in both large and small networks. It uses a technique known as *broadcasting*. When a device wants to use the network, it "listens" to see if someone else is using the network, and then it broadcasts. If another station is broadcasting, the messages will collide and each workstation will pause before attempting to broadcast again.

Have you ever been in a conversation where you and someone else have started "talking over each other?" One person will have to wait while the other one finishes what he or she has to say. In a nontechnical sense, this is what happens in a network that is broadcasting.

Under a broadcast network system, a single node will transmit information to all the other nodes at the same time. However, not all the nodes will pick up the message. In fact, only those nodes that have been addressed in the message will pick it up. Once the message is received, the receiving station will send an acknowledgment to the sending station.

Ethernet is fast. Its rated bandwidth—up to 100 megabits per second—makes it one of the fastest network solutions available. It can also accommodate extensive traffic. You can segment Ethernet networks into smaller logical networks to prevent overloading. Bridges can be used to filter traffic between networks, reducing contention for the cable and the impact of a cable break.

Ethernet is also versatile. When it first came out, Ethernet was a large, mysterious, and expensive yellow cable. Today, Ethernet can be run over:

- thick, durable cable,

- thin, lightweight 50-ohm coax (thin Ethernet),

- unshielded phone wire (twisted pairs),

- fiber-optic cable,

- any combination of the above that conforms to the Ethernet IEEE 802.3 specification.

Ethernet works with many types of networks. Software can be run over the same cable. You can have multiple PCs and PC file servers running Novell's NetWare software sharing the same cable with Macintosh equipment and several Sun Microsystems machines running UNIX. (Chapter 3 will explain UNIX and the different kinds of cable available.)

Hardware manufacturers have also worked hard to accommodate Ethernet. As a result, Ethernet supports the largest variety of devices of any network. Ethernet connections are offered as standard equipment on many workstations, including Sun workstations and DEC VAX computers.

The system also has drawbacks. It is more expensive than some solutions. The broadcast method can result in message collisions, which degrade performance. Broadcasting messages can also cause security problems. Because all information is broadcast to all the devices on the network, a hacker who gains access to part of the system can end up with access to the entire system.

FAST ETHERNET CARDS

With the use of special Network Interface Cards (NICs), such as those made by LAN Performance Labs, Intel, HP, DEC, Standard Microsystems,

NetWorth, and 3Com, you can run at 100 Mbps over Ethernet without using fiber optics. These cards cost 20% more than premium brand Ethernet cards, but they offer two to six times the performance. As with any new area of technology, however, things are still in a state of flux regarding 100-Mbps Ethernet. Specifically, there are currently two different standards for 100-Mbps LAN transmission, called 100BaseT and 100VG, respectively. These standards are not compatible with each other, so watch out! If you start with one type of NIC, you have to stay with it throughout your network. If you're seriously considering 100-Mbps Ethernet you also need to know that you will need special hubs in your network. Ordinary hubs simply won't handle the speed. And since many 100-Mbps NICs are dual-speed cards (they can operate at either 10 or 100 Mbps), the new type of hub comes in varieties that are either dedicated to the faster speed or can support more than one speed to the other as you migrate your LAN from slower to faster transmission speeds.

Whenever possible, consider using Fast Ethernet cards for your LAN.

T I P

Token Passing

Another important access method uses software to create a *token* (an electronic flag) that can be passed along a LAN from device to device. With this system, only the device with the token can transmit. A connected device will:

- Receive a token.

- Send its transmission.

- Pass the token to the next connected device.

While Ethernet provides random access, token passing guarantees every connected device access to the shared transmission system medium within a set period of time. Network operating system software will alter token passing according to a wide range of criteria and will provide for access priority.

On a token-ring LAN up to eight devices can be attached to a *Multistation Access Unit* (MAU). These are also known as *hubs*. Multiple hubs are connected together to create large multistation networks so that if a single workstation fails, the MAU will bypass it and maintain the ring of the network. MAUs usually have 8 or 16 ports, but they may have as few as 2. The IEEE's standard for token rings is the 802.5.

TOKEN RING SPECIFICATIONS

Maximum number of stations: 96

Maximum number of MAUs: 12

Maximum number of devices: 260

Maximum patch cable distance between a MAU and a station: 150 feet

Maximum patch cable distance connecting all MAUs: 400 feet

Maximum number of nodes supported: 260

In slightly more technical terms, token passing involves the transmission of a packet containing data and specialized status information that helps test for transmission errors. A packet on a token-passing system contains:

- Messages and commands, such as a request for service;
- Control codes for managing a session, such as codes that indicate communication errors and the need for retransmission;
- Data, the contents of a file.

When a device sends a packet to another device, one of three things happen:

- The receiving device is nonexistent or inactive and so the packet is never received.
- The receiving device exists, but the contents of the packet are not copied.
- The contents of the packet are copied.

You will learn more about token-passing systems, also known as *token rings*, in Chapter 3.

The major drawback of token-ring networking is that it is relatively slow (4 or 16 Mbps) when compared to the newer Fast Ethernet (100

Mbps) systems. As things stand right now, you pay more for token ring and get substantially less. This is not to say that things won't change as manufacturers devise new ways of speeding up token-ring technology, but for the time being, the field shows few signs of coming to life. If you are just starting out in networking, you should be aware that the area with the most activity right now is Ethernet.

Buyer's Guide: What to Look for in a System

- **What kind of server will you use?** NetWare 3.12, for example, requires at least a 386-based server, but you'll find that a 486 system is a better base on which to build.

- **How much RAM will the server need?** Realistically, you'll need at least 16 MB of RAM, and in many cases (such as NetWare 4.1 or Windows NT Server) 32 MB is the practical minimum.

- **What type of hard drive does it have?** Look for a large hard drive with 500 MB or more. Consider spending just a little more and getting a 1-gigabyte hard drive. Also, duplexed hard disks should be considered essential for any serious business LAN.

  Make sure you get a CD-ROM drive; almost all network operating systems come on CDs and you'll have to pay a large premium to have them shipped to you on floppy disks.

- **What is the expansion potential?** Be sure to choose a server that leaves you room to grow. You may consider tower cases because they typically offer numerous drive bays. However, you need to make sure that they are externally accessible to support CD-ROMs and tape backup systems. Because these accessories require additional power, look for a 300-watt or larger power supply with plenty of device connectors. Figure 2.3 shows a computer with potential for expansion.

- **What type of video does it have?** Because the server is handling the network operating system and won't be available for running applications, you can get by with *monochrome VGA*.

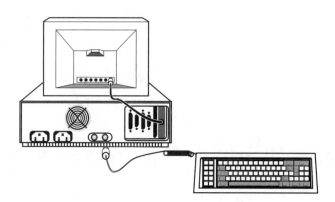

Figure 2.3 *Back of an IBM-type PC with expansion slots shown at the right side of the chassis.*

- **What type of workstation should you have?** Select workstations based on the requirements of the software you'll be using.

- **Will I need an extra expansion slot?** Yes, unless you opt for the portable or "pocket" type of network connection device, which connects externally to your PC via a parallel port.

- **What is the best networking operating system?** That depends on what you need. You can't go wrong with NetWare 3X for large complicated systems. On the other hand, if you have a modest number of DOS-only workstations and low cost or high flexibility are your primary concerns, you should at least consider LANtastic, Windows for Workgroups, or similar peer-to-peer networking systems.

- **What is the best cabling?** Currently, 10BaseT (unshielded twisted pair) cable is cost-effective and easy to install. It does, however, require a separate concentrator. Thin Ethernet used to be a good candidate but the price is now less competitive with 10BaseT. Also, if one Thin Ethernet cable segment is damaged or disconnected, the entire network may go down, and data may be lost. Fiber optics are also increasingly worthy of consideration where large databases are involved.

- **What options should I look at?** A backup system, such as a tape backup system, is essential. You should also consider disk duplexing. *Disk duplexing* uses two separate controllers to provide on-the-fly duplication of data. The cost of the hardware is rapidly shrinking and the cost of lost data from a damaged hard disk is enormous. Disk duplexing really should be considered essential, and for the money, it is probably some of the cheapest business insurance you'll ever buy.

- **What type of technical support do I need?** Make sure your vendor has competent and knowledgeable support personnel. For example, if you are using Novell products, make sure your vendor's staff includes Novell-trained Certified NetWare Engineers (CNEs). Then make sure your vendor's support lines will be available when you need them. Look for after-hours service if your plans include maintenance at nights and on weekends. Finally, remember that while on-site service is a welcome option available from most vendors, access software allows even faster diagnosis of many problems. If your vendor doesn't offer it as a standard network component, consider buying it as an option.

- **What else can I do to improve maintenance?** Consider doing your own remote support. Even if security policies at your company prevent you from taking advantage of a vendor's remote support options, you should consider installing a modem and the software to do your own support. Network administrators especially have easier lives if they can remotely troubleshoot their networks from home.

   Also, be sure to complete and return all warranty cards to their original equipment manufacturers. You should insist that all original floppy disks and manuals for your software be included in your shipment and that the software has been registered in your name so that you will be notified of upgrades and new products.

Putting It All Together

There is more to implementing a LAN system than just waking up one day and saying, "Wouldn't it be nice to have a LAN?" In some cases, you may not even need a LAN to accomplish your information goals. The first step, then, is to assess organizational needs. Some assessments start by looking at organizational problems; others focus on information needs alone.

Either way, the next step is to start thinking about what you really want. You need to look at the tricky issue of what you can afford, and you should begin to get an understanding of the hardware and software involved in a LAN, including the type of computer you will be using and the access method. Sometimes you may need to hire a consultant to help you with this process.

Glossary

broadcasting

Sending information from one node on a network to all nodes on a network.

consultant

Experts hired for relatively short periods to work on specific projects; paid by the day or by the hour.

contractor

An independent consultant.

cross-platform development

The process of creating programs that work identically on both Macs and PCs and whose files can be shared between users on both types of computers.

deterministic access method (DAM)

A method for connecting to a LAN that uses predefined rules and conditions to assign access priority to the various devices on a network.

disk duplexing

The use of two separate controllers and two separate hard disks to provide on-the-fly duplication of data.

Ethernet

A LAN access method allowing connected devices to transmit randomly. However, when more than one device attempts to transmit data using this system, both devices will wait for different periods before attempting data retransmission.

expansion slot	A connection inside a PC, into which you insert a network interface card, for example. Terms used to describe the different types of expansion slots (and cards) include: ISA, EISA, MCA, PCI, VESA, and NuBus (for Macintoshes).
hard costs	Costs associated with the elimination of a line item.
hypermedia	Use of text, data, graphics, video, and voice as elements in a hypertext system. With this system, all the forms of information are linked together so that a user can move easily from one to another.
mission critical statement	A management tool linking activities that make the difference between success and failure in a company with activities related to your current system.
monochrome VGA	Single color, or black and white monitor.
multistation access unit (MAU)	Also knows as hubs. On a token-ring LAN, a device for connecting up to eight workstations. MAUs usually have eight or 16 ports, but may have as few as two.
payback period	The amount of time it takes to recoup an investment.
present value	What a future amount of money is worth today.
random access method (RAM)	A method for connecting to a LAN that allows any connected device to request access to the shared medium at any time. Most office LANs depend on random access; others are deterministic.
Request for Proposal (RFP)	A tool for soliciting possible vendors to match a proposed solution. An RFP allows those providers sufficient information to give you a thorough estimate, while it permits you to compare competitive bids fairly.

return on investment (ROI)

A way of measuring the relative value of investments based on the current value of projected income or savings.

risk analysis

The art and science of weighing the benefits and costs of a decision under uncertain conditions.

soft cost

Cost for intangible benefits.

token

A software "flag" that manages access to a network's connecting medium.

token passing

An access method including software that manages access to a LAN's connecting medium. When a software token is passed around a network, only the device that holds the token is able to transmit data.

Windows

An operating environment developed by Microsoft that enables IBMs and clones to function with a graphical user interface.

Chapter 3

Cabling and Topology Issues

The cables you select, how you arrange those cables, and the nodes they connect are fundamental questions facing anyone planning a LAN. This chapter looks at the most popular kinds of cable, as well as wireless LANs.

A Basic LAN Cabling Tool Kit

If you are going to install your own LANs you should consider purchasing a set of very basic tools. Typical tools include:

- hammers

- screwdrivers

- pliers

- a drill (with several bits)

- wire cutters and strippers

- soldering iron

- crimpers for installing connectors to cables

- ohmmeter (used to measure the continuity of your cables)

- pair scanner (to check the integrity of twisted-pair wires)

- wall plates (so that the cable plugs into the connector)

Although each LAN is different, all LANs share a few basic patterns—also known as topologies—which are determined by the access method selected. This chapter describes the relationships between these basic patterns and the cables used.

Making the Connections

Cabling is important, even if only because LAN managers find that most of the hardware problems their users report involve cabling or cabling connections. In many cases, the cost of installing cabling and connectors for each workstation can exceed the cost of the workstation itself. Indeed, if you are having persistent problems with your LAN, the first place you would want to check is the cabling.

Cabling comes in three basic forms:

- twisted pair

- coaxial

- fiber optic

Twisted-Pair Cable

Twisted-pair cable consists of pairs of copper wire twisted together. The twisting is well thought out. Indeed, it is precisely calculated so that the wires carry more information further than they would if left as separate strands.

Why are the pairs of wires twisted? If they were not twisted, the long lengths of parallel wires would function as the two plates of a capacitor. Capacitors store electrical energy. Parallel wires would briefly store the rapidly changing electrical pulses that constitute a LAN's data flow. The untwisted wires would thus dampen the rapidly changing network signals the way a lake stores and smoothes out the tumbling water of the creeks that feed it. But twisting the wires around each other spoils their capacitance, allowing rapid electrical pulses applied to one end of a wire to show up as identical sharp voltage pulses at the other end. Unfortunately, even twisted wire pairs can't conduct signals more than a few hundred feet between computers. Figure 3.1 shows a twisted-pair wire.

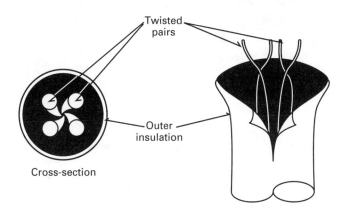

Figure 3.1 *A twisted-pair cable.*

How many pairs of cable can be twisted together? Twisted-pair cable is bundled in groups ranging from 4 to 3000 twisted pairs, although 25 pairs is standard in many local area networks. The wires are measured in American Wire Gauge (AWG) numbers, whose ranges are based on diameter. The most common types of LAN twisted-pair cables fall in the 22- to 24-gauge thickness range.

From a technical point of view, the cables are twisted together so that all wires face the same amount of noise or interference from the environment. This noise will then become part of the signal being transmitted. While twisting the wires together reduces this noise, it does not eliminate it.

When it was first introduced, twisted-pair cable for LANs could carry one megabit per second. Advances in the technology now allow information to travel much faster, at about 40 typewritten pages of text per second. The industry uses the standard known as *10BaseT*, which tracks information transmissions at 10 megabits per second. Figure 3.2 shows examples of both shielded and unshielded twisted-pair wires.

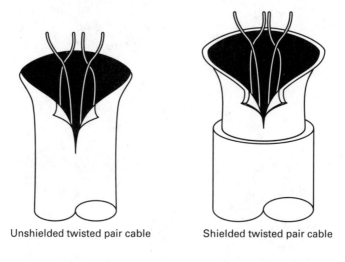

Unshielded twisted pair cable   Shielded twisted pair cable

Figure 3.2 *Examples of shielded and unshielded wires.*

A 1993 study by the Yankee Group marketing research firm found the following:

- It takes about three weeks to plan and execute a 30-node LAN move.

- More than seven out of ten problems in twisted-pair LANs are attributable to the wiring before the implementation of hubs, 35% after the hubs are implemented.

- More than 60% of the cost of moving to a LAN is the labor.

- It costs $500 or more *per node* to move an Ethernet unshielded twisted-pair (UTP) LAN.

Shielded and Unshielded

Two types of twisted-pair cables are used in LANs: shielded and unshielded.

Unshielded cable is commonly found in telephone wires. It tends to be much less expensive than shielded cables, which are more thoroughly insulated (shielded) from electrical interference than unshielded cable. However, unshielded twisted-pair cable is widely and successfully used. Some organizations have been able to use existing telephone wiring for LANs. However, this strategy requires extensive testing of the wiring to make sure it is reliable enough to carry computer information.

The lowest standard category of UTP currently sold is Category 5. Long the norm with 10-Mbps networks, it is also used for newer 100-Mbps systems. Category 5 cable is becoming increasingly common.

Manufacturers have specified twisted cable standards. IBM, for example, has recommended cables with four twisted pairs for any new installation. AT&T has specified shielded 24-gauge wire with two twists per foot. Under the AT&T system, one pair of wires is used to transmit data while the other is used to receive it.

Some analysts predict that sales of twisted-pair-based network products could soon eclipse other types of wire. Demand for twisted-pair wiring, particularly unshielded twisted cable, has grown rapidly in the last few years as organizations embrace structured wiring systems.

Coaxial Cable

Coaxial cable contains a single central wire surrounded by insulation and wire mesh. Coaxial cable for LANs is the same type of wire that delivers your favorite cable television shows. In general, coaxial cables are more expensive to buy, install, maintain, and work with than twisted-pair cable.

On the other hand, they can carry information farther than either unshielded or shielded twisted-pair cable. Coaxial supporters, who tend to ignore installation costs, also call it the most inexpensive solution available. This lower cost makes coaxial cable attractive to the growing number of small businesses and departments within larger organizations that are installing their first LANs. As a result, sales of coaxial cable have continued to grow at the modest rate of 10% each year.

Coaxial cable is also suitable for longer cable runs. For example, the 10Base2 standard for thin coaxial cable specifies that network segments be no longer than 100 meters without a repeater. Thick coaxial cable (also known as 10Base5), on the other hand, allows for runs up to 500 meters.

Coaxial cable has also enjoyed success abroad. In spite of its evident popularity, many analysts expect the domestic demand for coaxial-based products to dwindle over the next five to seven years. It is heavy, stiff, and expensive when compared with unshielded twisted-pair wiring. Nevertheless, its durability and simplicity appeal to users who would prefer to forget about their wiring and get on with their lives as soon as installation is completed. Either way you look at it, coaxial cable is still a major part of the LAN market and should be expected to remain so for the foreseeable future. Figure 3.3 shows an example of a coaxial cable.

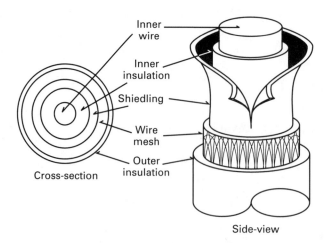

Figure 3.3 *An example of coaxial cable.*

Thin coaxial cable is less durable than the thick version. However, thin coaxial cable is also less expensive and more flexible. Thin cabling is recommended when changes of LAN equipment and moves are frequent, such as in office buildings. Thick coaxial cable is often used in such rugged environments as factories and machine shops, especially when workstations are far apart and when cables need to pass near major sources of electromagnetic energy. Your average welding apparatus, for example, will generate enough interference to render most other types of computer communications cable virtually useless. An exception is the electrically immune cable we will talk about next: *fiber optics.*

BNC connectors are used to connect thin coaxial cable networks. The *B* stands for bayonet, and the connector twists on with a simple half-turn not unlike a bayonet being fixed to a rifle. BNC connectors come in four forms:

- *BNC connectors*, which attach directly to the cable

- *BNC-T connectors*, which provide cable attachments to the network interface card

- *BNC barrel connects*, which connect two cable segments

- *BNC terminators*, which have resistors to terminate the coaxial cable

If you don't know where to find these tools in your community you can search through several popular catalogs. Two very popular ones are: AMP Corporation, (800) 522-6752, and Jensen Company, (602) 968-6231.

Patch Cables

Token ring networks use special pieces of cable known as *patch cables.* They extend the distance between a workstation and a MAU (multiaccess unit) device, or they can be used to cable two or more MAU devices together. Patch cables are available in 30-, 75-, and 150-foot lengths. They are IBM type 6 cables with IBM system cabling connectors on each end.

Using Telephone Wires

Working with telephone wires frequently requires the use of registered jacks. The two most common are the RJ11 and the RJ45 (RJ stands for "registered jack"). The RJ45 is similar to the voice grade RJ11, but has more points of contact. The RJ45 is more often used in LANs.

ETHERNET CABLING

The three most popular Ethernet cables are 10BaseT, 10Base5, and 10Base2. The *10* refers to a frequency of 10 Mbps. The *base* means baseband, a transmission system where the entire bandwidth of the cable system is used for the single signal. The last number stands for the length between repeaters, stated in hundreds of meters. Thus, for 10Base2, the maximum length between repeaters is 200 meters, and for 10Base5 it's 500 meters.

Dos and Don'ts for Laying Coaxial Cable

Do:

- make gentle curves (with a radius no longer than 2 inches)
- hang or lay the coaxial cable out
- keep the cable round, especially at bends and taps
- tape barrel connections if there is any chance they will contact metal
- pick cables up by their plastic insulation when connecting two cable ends

Don't:

- staple coax
- make tight bends in coaxial cable
- lay coaxial cable on top of light fixtures
- place the cable near power lines, high-power devices, or fluorescent lights
- pick up two unconnected ends of coax, one in each hand

T I P

Moisture can migrate through cable braid as if it were a candlewick. The fine copper wires of the braid will corrode and then crumble apart, creating an "open" in the outer shield. To prevent this problem, never use a piece of cable that has damage in the outer cover that exposes the braid area to the atmosphere.

Fiber Optics

Although some day fiber-optic cable may be the industry standard, today it is the least common type. This form of cable contains a hair-thin strand of optically pure plastic fiber surrounded by special shielding and insulation. The optical fibers carry pulses of light as opposed to the bursts of electricity handled by twisted-pair or coaxial wires. A fiber-optic network uses either a laser or light-emitting diode (LED) to translate electrical signals into light pulses and then sends the light signal through the core portion of the cable. Optical repeaters are often used along the path to amplify the signal so that it arrives at its destination at full strength. At the receiving end of the cable, the signal is translated back into an electrical pulse with the same shape as the light pulse.

In the long run, this type of technology will eclipse wires because fiber-optic cable can carry more information further in less space, it never rusts or corrodes, it is completely free of all kinds of interference from other sources of electrical noise, and it is remarkably hard for anyone to tap into. Witness the fact that most of the nation's long distance telephone companies now use optical fiber for their backbone networks, and even many local phone companies are gradually upgrading their wiring systems with fiber. Quietly, laser-based communication has already arrived in our lives. The next question is whether, and how soon, you and I will be handling it with the same degree of casualness that we deal with copper wire.

The biggest drawback of fiber-optic cable, at this point, is its expense. Maintenance can also be much more costly. When a fiber-optic cable breaks, major problems can result, because one fiber-optic cable may be carrying as much information as hundreds of twisted pairs of copper wire. A break in a fiber-optic cable could affect a large number of users.

Prices, however, could be decreasing. Until recently, fiber-optic networks for PCs have used strands of glass as the transfer medium. However, a plastic cable developed by Codenoll Technology and the Packard Electric Division of General Motors potentially offers a promise to save dollars and headaches in fiber-optic installations.

The price of fiber-optic adapters is also decreasing. Figure 3.4 shows a timeline for fiber-optic installation milestones. Indeed, some low-cost fiber-optic adapters have already won press coverage for saving taxpayer money at the United States Department of Agriculture's Facilities Management Division. Originally, 16 of the nodes on an 80-plus-node fiber-optic Ethernet local area network in Washington, D.C., were connected to adapters from Raylan Corporation that cost between $495 and $895. Eventually, all of the workstations on the LAN will have the Raylan board. The USDA chose this system in order to minimize downtime in its operation responsible for:

- running equipment inventory and maintenance databases
- a database of security photos of all department employees
- managing computer-aided design files of items such as floor plans

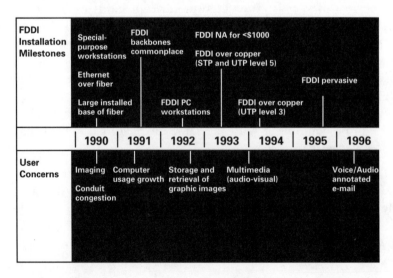

Figure 3.4 *Timeline for fiber distributed data interface (FDDI).*

The Who, What, When, and Where of Cabling

Many networks, such as Ethernet systems, actually can use both thin and thick coaxial cable and twisted-pair cables. Some network interface cards even have the external connectors and on-board electronics to handle any kind of cabling you decide to attach. As mentioned already, twisted-pair wiring for Ethernet has increased in popularity as the price of equipment has dropped and reliability has increased. Nevertheless, the exact type you choose may not be as important as making sure your cabling is something you can live with for at least several years. Cabling is a headache, it's expensive, and it's not something you want to have to do again anytime soon. This is one area where you really need to sit yourself down and try to come up with an honest assessment of what you're going to need a year from now versus what you need today.

If your growth rate is high and you expect it to be sustained, buying only what you need to cover today's emergencies may be short-sighted. It is a sure way to guarantee that you'll have to do the whole exercise all over again in the near to midterm future.

If you really feel that your needs are stable, you don't expect a lot of growth, and you are looking into LANs for their efficiency and convenience rather than as a way of managing expansion, then it makes less sense to buy more capacity than you can use now.

Whose Cabling to Use

Most LAN offerings come with specific recommendations regarding the types of cable to use. Some systems even come with cable. As a rule of thumb, these cables are best suited to a particular system. However, they may not fit your overall cabling plan. Third-party vendors can fill in. In these cases, the convenience of vendor-supplied cable needs to be weighed against issues of cost and compatibility.

Most work sites, especially those with LANs, have some cable already installed. Is this cable reliable enough to support critical LAN applications? Does the existing cable have sufficient capacity? The answers to these questions will determine whether you use existing cable or replace it.

Where to Put the Cabling?

Your cable installer may recommend the use of surface raceways, which allow cables to run along the outer edges of common floors covered by metal conduits that are attached at the room's floorboards. This method is popular because it provides protection from electromagnetic interference. However, surface raceways are difficult to move or modify if a network expands or changes. Figure 3.5 shows a surface raceway in cross section and in a typical installation.

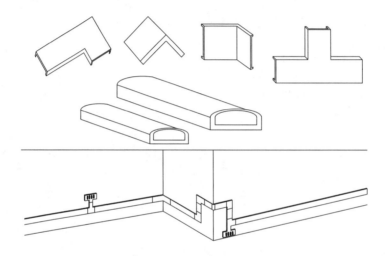

Figure 3.5 *A surface raceway.*

Cable can also be installed under floors or over ceilings. Under-floor cabling, which is usually housed in steel ducts or trenches, is difficult to tap and is resistant to breaks and cuts. Over-ceiling cabling competes with air conditioning, lighting, and power conduits that sometimes squeeze out this popular inexpensive method.

Who is Responsible for Cabling?

If you are using telephone wire (which is what twisted-pair cabling is), why not hire telephone installers to do your LAN cabling? As logical as that sounds, the fact is that telephone installers are not inherently endowed with the knowledge of how to design or implement a high-frequency LAN using either unshielded or shielded twisted-pair cable. The best solution is to hire a LAN installation specialist.

Ultimately, cabling is another responsibility placed on the shoulders of the network manager. A network manager must be versatile enough to meet the changing demands of the job. In one day, this administrator may do everything from designing the network to fixing cable problems. As networks become more critical to a company's business line functions, networks must be managed more efficiently. Planning becomes increasingly important as managers must anticipate growth and performance problems, rather than react to catastrophes and failures. Often, a network manager must work with:

- LAN vendors
- cabling vendors
- cable installation firms
- individual users
- building owners or managers

As far as cabling is concerned, the network manager's job is to be responsible for:

- installing
- moving
- changing
- inventorying
- regularly testing cables
- resolving cabling problems

In most areas, cabling that links the floors of a building is the responsibility of the building owner or manager, and cabling that links facilities on a floor is the responsibility of individual tenant organizations or work groups.

Cable Type

What kind of wire will you buy? If you buy coaxial cable at $.30/foot you will get high resistance to interference from machinery, but the cable is thick, susceptible to kinking, and harder to "run." You can choose unshielded twisted-pair cabling at $.15/foot, which is also easy to fold. But twisted-pair cable can pick up noise from heavy machinery, microwave ovens, and power lines that reduce its suitability for use in, say, a steel mill. For a couple of dollars a foot you could run fiber-optic cable, transparent threads conducting light pulses that are totally immune to electrical interference but expensive to connect to.

Cable Testing

Cabling is one of the most sensitive areas in LANs today. Between 60% and 80% of LAN downtime, *LAN Technology* estimates, is cable-related; therefore, you've got to learn to face cable problems and rope them in quickly before they tie you in knots.

Cables should be pretested before they are installed to help you avoid problems later. In addition to pretesting, each piece of cable should be visually inspected before installation. Once you have installed cable, solving problems becomes more expensive and time-consuming.

Once the cable is installed, it needs to be tested again. Later on, it will need to be tested regularly for problems, such as breaks and faulty insulation. LAN users should turn to suppliers and managers for help in this process.

What about grounding? A *ground* is an electrical path designed to disperse high-voltage electrical spikes, usually by routing them into the earth. Grounding requirements can also be important. The documentation for each product will reveal any special grounding requirements. You should be aware, however, that every cabling system should be grounded at only one point. Multiple grounding points can create electrical interference that defeats your cabling's shielding.

Cable length is also an important consideration. Cable that is too long can cause stations not to come up at all, or they may come up but crash frequently. Other important considerations are cable weight and placement.

Support should be provided every 15 to 20 feet to prevent sagging; cable sags decrease a cable's reliability and life. You also need to make certain that cable installers don't set up cables to support the weight of connected devices, such as splitters. Each device needs to either rest on or be attached to something that can support it, such as a wall or duct.

To reduce the likelihood of accidental groundings, shorts, or transient electrical problems, make sure that all cable ends are properly sealed and terminated.

This type of prevention can help you avoid time-consuming problems. Shorts and other such problems are often difficult to pinpoint.

Troubleshooting

A variety of tools can be used when troubleshooting or certifying cable, including:

- digital volt meter (DVM)
- time domain reflectometers (TDR)
- oscilloscope

The most basic tool available to a troubleshooter is the digital volt meter (DVM). A typical DVM measures the presence of a continuous connection from one end of a cable to the other and the ease with which electricity can flow through the cable. It does this by showing the electrical resistance of each leg of your network, and it is used to measure the resistance of a cable or to determine continuity.

The TDR works like a radar system; it sends its signal down a cable and then collects and interprets returning reflections. The basic TDR can be used to:

- Measure lengths of cable (which is important when certifying that a cable conforms to a specification)
- Find opens and shorts
- Provide an attenuation measurement of the cable (when coupled with an oscilloscope)

The oscilloscope is a graphical device that measures signal voltage (vertical axis) per unit of time (horizontal axis). The oscilloscope can be used to display reflections returning from the TDR impulse signal. While the TDR displays the length of the cable, the oscilloscope displays:

- transceiver locations
- shorts
- crimps
- opens
- other impedance mismatches on that cable segment
- voltage-level data that can be used to calculate attenuation

How Major Vendors are Addressing Cabling Issues

IBM, AT&T, and DEC have all developed unique responses to customer needs for unified wiring and distribution. IBM Cabling System, for example, is designed primarily for star networks (for a description of star networks and other topologies, read the next section). One of its strong points is that the connectors are *genderless*, meaning that any connector can be plugged into any other connector. The system uses two different types of cable, one for data communications (IBM Type I) and one that accommodates both data and voice (Type II).

The AT&T wiring system emphasizes unshielded twisted-pair copper wire used in telephone systems. Sometimes, however, it uses fiber-optic cable to link these twisted-pair wires. The connectors use existing connector technologies. AT&T has also developed special jacks. In the final analysis, AT&T also emphasizes star configuration.

Digital Equipment Corporation (DEC) has developed systems that rely on Ethernet, running coaxial or fiber-optic cable, to provide all connections. The topology emphasized is a bus/star hybrid. Every floor in a building uses a star, but floors are connected with a bus. Cables for voice and data transmission are separated physically. DEC systems do use at least one nonstandard connector.

Wireless LANs

Wireless LANs are actually a type of product emerging from more than one line of technological developments. Some of these LANs use systems based on radio technology. Others depend on infrared light, invisible to the human eye under usual working conditions. Wireless LANs can be more expensive per connection, but they can:

- Provide interim additions to a larger, cabled LAN
- Create an easily activated backup LAN
- Satisfy the curiosity of anyone who wants to experiment with new technology
- Service users seeking portability

Data Switches

A *data switch* is a device linking terminals, computers, and other computer devices to a host computer. Data switches are basically concentrator devices. A data switch has between 8 and 64 ports; each data switch has a built-in microprocessor. Data switches are connected through the serial ports of computers. The data switch manufacturer usually provides software. However, data switches can also use programs such as LapLink. Data switches are available at many computer stores and from catalogs, including:

- Western Telematic, (800) 854-7226
- Buffalo Box, Inc., (503) 585-3414
- Computer Friends, (800) 829-9991

Choices and Costs

When all is said and done, you cannot overestimate the importance of cable planning. Although LANs tend to be less costly than mainframe solutions, expenses do add up. In today's economically pressed times, costs often determine what systems will be purchased. However, both long-term and short-term consequences of any solution need to be taken into consideration.

LAN managers like to joke about having "cable pits," instead of closets or drawers for cables and connectors. Some of these pits, they say, are so large that small pets can get lost in them. The point is that cabling is difficult, and wireless LANs are still in the development phase. Meanwhile, most managers have large collections of cables and connectors.

Other Considerations

In addition to costs and cable type, a unified cabling plan should ultimately take the following factors into consideration:

- user and contractor safety
- facility security
- applicable regulations
- network performance needs
- availability of rights-of-way in need areas
- room for growth

Planning for growth is especially important because costs tend to increase as the LAN grows.

You should also always remember that a LAN may not be the ideal solution for your organization. As you recall, organizations with strong needs for information-sharing over wide areas should consider MANs and WANS. These choices, however, only increase the need for cabling. On the other hand, if your organization doesn't need a LAN, there is no sense in going through with cable planning. Never be afraid to at least look at alternative solutions.

Wireless connectors are only one way to link portable computers to a LAN. If you feel uncomfortable with wireless technology, you can still find solutions allowing you to integrate laptop computers to your LAN. For example, you can attach a printer port adapter to your laptop computer. The connections take only a few minutes and add only a few ounces to the traveling ensemble. Remote control software, which we will discuss later, lets remote users access information, manipulate it, and produce usable results.

Topologies: Making the Best Arrangements

Network architecture or *topology* describes the way a network is set up. The three most common configurations are the *star*, a variant of the star called the *ring*, and the *bus*.

The Star

Of all the topologies, the star topology is one of the oldest. This system roughly parallels a telephone system. In a telephone system, telephone calls from one customer to another are handled by a central switching station. With a LAN star topology, all messages are routed through a central hub. It is not surprising that AT&T, the telephone company, was one of the first to develop this type of product with its *STARLAN*.

With a star topology, adding new workstations is as easy as adding a network interface card and connecting a wire to the central computer. (The biggest drawback of this system, on the other hand, is that if the central server has difficulties, the entire network will malfunction.) The central server also lets you diagnose all records functions easily by analyzing all workstation messages and listing files used by each node. Another advantage is that the network manager has the ability to give certain nodes higher priority than others. The central hub will search for signals from these higher-priority workstations before recognizing other nodes. For networks where a few key users demand immediate response from on-line inquiries, this feature is essential.

Clustered Star

This topology consists of several stars linked together. Although the stars are linked, the failure of one star does not result in the failure of the entire network. Clustered stars are becoming increasingly common, in many cases replacing central server stars. Figure 3.6 shows a basic star topology.

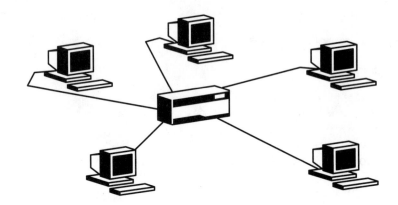

Figure 3.6 *Star topology.*

Hubs

Hubs are the central location for the connection of computer stations in a star configuration. There are many types of hubs; that topic alone could fill an entire book. There are two basic types, passive and active. *Passive hubs* are small boxes with just a few ports for the connection of the computer station in a star configuration. A passive hub might also be a wiring block. It does not require an electrical connection. On the other hand, an *active hub* will have more points and will regenerate signals from one device to another. Hubs make structured wiring possible and accommodate different networking options, including Ethernet, token ring, FDDI, and wide area network connections, such as Frame Relay, SMDS, and ATM. Many of the more advanced hubs have built-in management features.

Most high-end hubs have their own microprocessors that can run programs to track data packets and errors and store the information in a specialized type of database called a *management information base* (MIB).

The Bus Topology

No, a bus topology is not shaped like an autobus. A *bus* is just another name for a single master cable that carries all traffic. The idea is that the

LAN is configured around a single cable; it even predates the star topology. However, you can think of an autobus and configure a bus topology with the file server as the autobus "driver" and the PCs and workstations with their peripherals lined up behind it as "passengers." The idea is that the file server controls all the other computers (bus passengers). The problem, however, is that devices on a bus network need to be far enough apart so that electrical interference will not disrupt accurate communications. In some cases, amplifiers are used to help signals complete their journey. The problem is that a single bad workstation in the daisy-chain can derail the bus.

Bus networks are popular because they are simple. You can add new stations to them, and they can be managed centrally or use file servers. Figure 3.7 shows a basic bus topology.

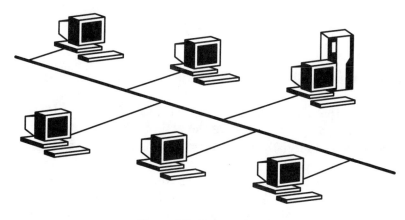

Figure 3.7 *Bus topology.*

The Ring

Token Ring networks use a topology with the physical appearance of a star but they operate under different rules. Electrically, signals travel from one workstation to the next by first passing through the central hub. In this sense, the topology is like a star. Nevertheless, the signals only transit through the hub, they are not processed there. The actual destination of the signal is the next workstation, where it is captured and acted upon. So, even though it looks like a star, the ring is actually a separate kind of network topology. Figure 3.8 shows a basic ring topology.

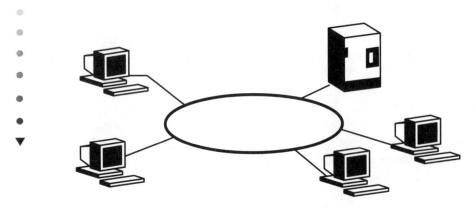

Figure 3.8 *Ring topology.*

Token rings now routinely use active hubs. Passive hubs, once very popular with token ring users, are becoming less popular.

T I P

A Final Caution

Do not make the mistake of thinking that just because the LAN industry has standards, you no longer have the ability to make your own choices. Salespeople seem especially adept at promoting personal biases as industry standards. Don't be fooled: you really can mix and match cabling styles with different network speeds and network operating system software. Many salespeople, for example, do not realize the independence of wiring decisions, and will insist that "LANtastic will only work with Ethernet coaxial bus cabling." So potential customers pass up LANtastic, thinking they can't get the hardiness of a star wiring system with that simple network software. Or they think that they can't use a star wiring pattern with Ethernet. The truth is that peer-type networking systems can provide the hardiness of a star wiring system and, yes, you *can* use a star wiring pattern with Ethernet.

Putting It All Together

Cabling is the biggest cause of hardware problems. The cost of installing cabling and connectors for each workstation can exceed the cost of the workstation itself. With that in mind, let's recap some earlier points.

- Cabling comes in three basic forms: twisted pair, coaxial, and fiber optic.
- Cablers must make thoughtful decisions about topology. For those systems that are not wireless (and most are not), the most common topologies are the star and the bus.

How many wires will you run between your computers? Will you try to minimize the amount of wire used by daisy-chaining your computers together? If you do, you have chosen a bus topology for your LAN. Daisy-chained computers minimize wiring installation costs, but it is hard to figure out where a wiring problem is coming from when every computer is on the same long wire. A single cable break anywhere in the system can bring the whole system to a halt.

Will you run a separate wire from each computer to a central hub? Then you have chosen a star topology that requires more wire but gives each computer its own private line. When a single computer or wire goes bad in a star topology network, no other computers are affected since only one spoke out from the hub is defective.

Glossary

American Wire Gauge (AWG) numbers	Standard measurement for the thickness of electrical wires—ranges are based on the wire's diameter.
attenuation	Measurement of power loss as the signal traverses the cable.
BNC	Connector used on coaxial cables.
bus	A network in which all nodes are attached to a single cable in a daisy-chain pattern.
capacitance	Usually measured in picofarads per foot or meter, this measures the energy absorbed by the cable.
Category 5	A reference to the type of twisted-pair cable increasingly used in 100BaseT networks.
certifying	Establishing the integrity and adequacy of a piece of cable.

characteristic impedance	Measured in ohms; a measurement of the cable's resistance to electric current at an operational frequency.
clustered star	A topology of several stars linked together.
coaxial cable	A network wiring medium with a metal core surrounded by grounding material and insulation.
crosstalk	Measured in decibels; a measurement of the induced signal (noise) in a wire pair from another wire pair in the same cable sheath.
daisy-chain	Connecting each computer directly to one on either side so that each computer in a network is attached to the same wire.
data switch	A device linking terminals, computers, and other computer devices to a host computer.
digital volt meter (DVM)	A tool used to measure the resistance of a cable or to determine continuity.
fiber optic	A media used for networks, using slender glass thread surrounded by cushioning and insulating material; carries network signals at very high speeds.
ground	An electrical path designed to disperse high-voltage electrical spikes, usually by routing them into the earth.
hub	The central connector for a LAN, such as in a star topology.
management information base (MIB)	A specialized type of database used to store network information.
metropolitan area network (MAN)	A LAN-like network between several different buildings.
ohmmeter	Device used to measure the continuity of your cables.

oscilloscope	A graphical device that measures signal voltage (vertical axis) per unit of time (horizontal axis).
passive hub	A device on a token ring network that receives signals from one workstation for forwarding on to a destination workstation.
ring topology	A circular bus topology.
star	A network configuration where all devices have a direct path to the hub.
surface raceway	Device allowing cables to run along the outer edges of common floors covered by metal conduits attached at the room's floorboards.
time domain reflectometer (TDR)	Device that measure lengths of cable and finds opens and shorts.
10BaseT	The industry standard that tracks information transmissions at 10 megabits per second.
100BaseT	The industry standard that tracks information transmission at 100 megabits per second.
topology	Basic network architecture or design.
twisted-pair wiring	A popular and inexpensive way of linking devices in a LAN. There are two types of twisted-pair wiring: shielded and unshielded. Unshielded cable is commonly found in telephone wires. Shielded cable is more thoroughly insulated, or shielded, from electrical interference and is more reliable.
wide area network (WAN)	A LAN-like network that covers a big geographic area.

Chapter

4

The Network Operating System

The *network operating system* (NOS) can intercept requests for data from the programs you are running and pull the information over the network cables from another computer. For example, a good NOS can make your LAN neighbor's disk drive appear as if it were attached to your computer. It can also collect your print jobs in a few seconds and dole them out slowly over the network wires to a remote printer.

You can add software to almost every NOS to set up electronic mailboxes or share a fax/modem. There are dozens of add-on packages to help you audit who's doing what on the network or to help you look in on another user's screen. Chapter 6 covers the major vendors offering NOS software. This chapter focuses on general background.

Operating System Types

The computer's operating system software coordinates all of the computer's functions. The operating system is like the conductor of a symphony, making sure that all the components work together. A conductor works with sheet music and instruments; a computer works with hardware and software. Without an operating system, your desktop computer would not be able to run any applications.

There are many types of operating systems. In the past, for example, IBM and Macintosh computers have had very different operating systems. In most cases, Macintosh software could not read IBM-compatible software and vice versa. The Mac has always had a more "complete" operating system than the IBM PC. Graphics programs have taken longer to develop on the PC, for example, because PC software packages have had to do more of the picture drawing themselves.

PC-Type Operating Systems

In most cases, IBM-compatible computers use DOS (disk operating system) software. In many cases, this software is manufactured by Microsoft and is known as MS-DOS. There is also a popular version developed by Digital Research, formerly known as DR-DOS (now known as Novell DOS). Novell purchased DR-DOS in 1992, thereby providing DR-DOS with the advantages of Novell's Network NOS. In any event, there are several versions of DOS out there, and these programs are updated occasionally.

Ordinary DOS, however, is not the most advanced operating system available to PC-type microcomputers. Many advanced LAN products are based on IBM's OS/2. The OS/2 operating system includes many network-related functions that DOS does not include. In addition, OS/2 takes advantage of the added capabilities of the 80386, 80486, and Pentium chips. These new chips allow OS/2 to:

- manage large amounts of system memory
- support communication among computing processes
- perform more than one task at a time (multitasking)

Windows NT, as mentioned in Chapter 2, is an advanced 32-bit operating system that works on several processors. Windows NT's ability to fully access 32-bit processors allows it to work with larger numbers, memory addresses, and instructions. This means that *overall throughput*, the combination of processor performance, data transfer, and memory access, will improve. Windows NT was also created with several network-friendly capabilities built in and is thus considered a good candidate for all-around office and network applications.

Between the NOS and the network interface card lies a small piece of software that handles the job of relaying small packets of data over the wires. That small network driver is called the *IPX driver* on Novell networks and the *NETBIOS driver* on most other DOS LANs. A recent trend is for Novell/DR-DOS and MS-DOS to include IPX drivers as part of every DOS package they sell.

One of the key advantages of using DOS-based software is that it can be installed quickly and easily by anyone who takes the time to study the documentation and has a feel for software installation.

Non-DOS Systems

The hard disk drives of servers on LANs using central servers, however, may not be running under DOS. They may be formatted under a non-DOS network operating system specific to the LAN vendor. This operating system will typically handle larger hard disks than DOS, find files faster, and provide greater security than a standard DOS hard disk.

Meanwhile, Apple has continued to develop the Macintosh operating system, which includes a simple LAN called AppleTalk. Other desktop computing systems use an operating system called UNIX, which was originally designed for large mainframe systems. LAN software for UNIX is sophisticated and sometimes expensive.

Although operating systems differ in how they work to present information to users, they all perform the same types of functions.

Network Utilities

Operating systems provide tools, also known as utilities, to make better use of your computers. These include tools for:

- listing files
- formatting disks
- copying files
- moving files
- clearing the display screen

Operating systems also provide a range of services providing access to application programs, files, printers, and other resources.

Operating Systems: A Competitive Market

The world of operating systems is very competitive. The major vendors are always upgrading their operating systems in order to outdo their competitors. When one operating system is upgraded, all the others follow suit. No one wants to be left behind. For example, when System 7.0, the long-awaited advanced operating system software for Apple Macintosh computers finally came out, it was viewed as giving the company a competitive edge. IBM retaliated by upgrading OS/2 version 1.0 to OS/2 version 2.0. Analysts also point out that OS/2 version 2 was a competitive response to Microsoft's development of Windows, its popular graphical user interface, and new MS-DOS versions.

IBM's OS/2 Warp operating system can run Microsoft Windows applications, but unlike Windows shells and enhancement utilities, it is a true alternative operating system with a complete user environment of its own.

T I P

Moving to OS/2 requires a major commitment, but it is an alternative that many Windows users should consider.

Network Operating System: Your LAN's Heart and Soul

A simple network operating system will work with the operating system of each individual workstation and will provide the missing abilities a network needs. For example, when you use a database management program on a LAN, your PC operating system will act as it did before being connected to the LAN. However, the network operating system will function in tandem with the PC operating system. Now you can keep a single network-license copy of your database management program on the file server, and it can be shared by everyone on the LAN.

Network Operating Systems: A Key to LAN Connectivity

Some LAN system software is written for specific applications, such as control of various processes in a manufacturing facility. However, most LAN operating systems are general-purpose. They are written to support a variety of applications and operating systems on many different PCs and workstations. In other words, the best network operating system provides services and performs tasks with only minimal changes to the ways the hardware worked before being connected to a LAN.

In the old days of LANs, most operating systems were closed. Closed LANs are typically restricted to equipment and software from one or a few vendors. For example, an Apple Macintosh user working among IBM PC users had to choose between the Mac machine and participation in the IBM-compatible LAN.

Today, however, most developers have worked to promote connectivity and at least some degree of openness. For example, Novell's NetWare was originally written for IBM PCs and clones. However, it was enhanced to include Macintosh support in 1988. Since then, it has become progressively more "open." In the same manner, TOPS, originally a network almost exclusively for Macintosh LANs, now also supports IBM-compatible PCs.

Network Operating System Trends

Object-oriented programming is—and promises to continue to be—a hot topic in the management of network software. Object-oriented programming uses data objects; each object knows how to respond to a set of commands that can be given to it. A growing number of proponents of object-oriented programming say that it becomes a more valuable tool as LANs grow large and become more and more interconnected. The proponents say object-oriented programming provides a basis for distributing management tasks across the enterprise and scaling functionality upward from workgroups. Software developers say it will be easier to develop network applications and to reuse and share code with object-oriented programming (this is already the case with other software). On the other hand, critics disagree and say that a platform's capabilities do not rely on the programming techniques being used.

Another hot topic is multiprotocol support. The trend is to have operating systems that support an increasing number of protocols. Finally, another important trend is to have more software providing more detailed monitoring of network activities.

Network Management Tools

A network manager may want to record who uses what files and when. Network management tools also assign passwords, monitor performance, and name storage areas. Products exist to:

- report on server utilization
- implement security
- test cables
- monitor every device attached to the LAN

Network Management Stations

Many networks have special controlling devices that track packet transmissions and monitor connections and error conditions. A network management station (NMS) gathers information about these processes and stores it on disks. That way, special problems can be detected.

Integral to the functioning of network management stations is some method, or *protocol*, for gathering statistical network information. One of the most widely accepted of these protocols is called the Simple Network Management Protocol (SNMP). SNMP is the protocol that the network management stations and various network devices use to exchange information.

Backup Management

Backup is important in the event of a network failure. Without adequate backup you can lose every piece of data on your system. By having an adequate backup system you can ensure that only a minimum amount of work will have to be redone if there is a failure. That is why many operating systems work directly with storage systems designed for creating backup files.

The most sophisticated backup systems can record network archives to other media in addition to disks. Many work with tape drives, optical disks, videotape, and audiotape. SitBack for Windows, for example, supports floppy disks as backup media, in addition to hard disks, removable disks, network file servers, and optical tape drives. Advanced systems will automatically create and update copies of programs and user files in addition to system information, such as which users have which rights and privileges.

LAN Managers and LAN Backups

Disaster recovery, according to a recent survey by *Datamation*, is a hot topic among corporate information systems managers. Concern for backups is on the rise. Among the survey's findings:

- 91% of the managers surveyed have disaster recovery plans in place
- 86% have formal documentation of such plans
- 56% say their systems are sufficiently protected
- 91% use off-site tape storage as a part of their plan
- 32% use disaster recovery storage
- 39% emphasize backup communication networks

Causes for such breakdowns range from severe weather conditions resulting in physical damage of systems to disk crashes and other equipment failures. Disk crashes are common. However, communications failures can be caused by more exotic factors, such as work crews cutting lines and completely disabling remote sites. Natural disasters, such as floods, and less dramatic problems such as lightning, can also cause power outages and physical damage to systems and may prevent personnel from accessing facilities.

In many cases, MIS organizations are required by government regulations, company auditors, or insurance companies to have disaster recovery plans. Disaster recovery plans may be as simple as having formal procedures for whom to notify in the case of problems, or it may necessitate keeping daily backup tapes at an off site-facility.

POWER MANAGEMENT

LANs often use backup power systems and have sophisticated network operating systems that can communicate directly with these systems. An *uninterruptible power supply (UPS)* provides batteries and circuits that activate these backup systems when regular power fades or disappears. Figure 4.1 shows a typical power backup system. When a UPS finds a condition that makes normal power unreliable, it:

1. activates its batteries;

2. sends a message to the LAN's operating system, warning of an imminent loss of power;

3. begins getting users off the network;

4. starts to update all backup copies of network information; and

5. may eventually shut down the LAN if normal power is not restored.

Resource Management

Resource management software performs functions such as keeping track of the number of times users access files. The more sophisticated resource management tools track traffic levels and other performance issues. This information helps managers allocate resources. For example, you wouldn't want to schedule a big print job during a period of peak demand. Some operating systems include software that can predict the effect of network growth or server failures on overall network performance. Others allow you to add software that makes these predictions.

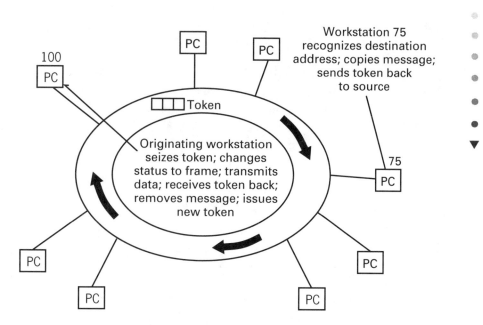

Figure 4.1 *Uninterruptible power supply.*

STEPS TOWARD BUYING AND EXPANDING A LOCAL AREA NETWORK

1. **Select a Network Operating System (NOS).** If you have no LAN product commitment, the first product to be selected should be the NOS. Selection is normally based on the features the NOS offers and the services it can provide to users. Interoperability issues arise only if the user has some systems installed and must ensure NOS compatibility.

2. **Select a topology.** Next you select the LAN topology, media, and access control scheme. These selections can be made by examining each of the options the NOS supports and relating them to network media issues, such as building wiring limitations, distance between workstations, and performance. LANs in a small area are suited to star networks. In contrast, it is easier to daisy-chain a bus network throughout a large building.

3. **Select a cable type.** Typical small office networks can get by with simple twisted-pair wires. Buildings with long wire runs and lots of machinery call for coaxial or fiber-optic cable.

4. **Select network interface cards.** Don't buy a network interface card that can only be used with one NOS.

N O T E Microsoft and IBM are among the companies making network operating software installation easier than ever. CD-ROM installation is the best because users do not have to swap dozens of floppies. The Warp version of OS/2 has a new one-button install routine.

Putting It All Together

The heart and soul of a network is its operating system software. Unfortunately, even today, not all computer operating systems are compatible with each other or with all network operating systems. There is, however, a movement toward more open systems. Despite the differences between disk operating systems, the latest NOSes can share files among otherwise incompatible computers.

A good rule of thumb is that you will probably need additional software any time you link a few PCs. Much of this additional software will be used to manage the LAN.

Glossary

American Standard Code for Information Interchange (ASCII)
A binary code for data in communications, most minicomputers, and all personal computers.

NETBIOS
The standard set of enhancements for IBM PC-DOS and compatible operating systems.

object-oriented programming
A method off writing programs that uses data objects, each knowing how to respond to a set of commands that can be given to it, instead of writing programs by using a specialized language, or code.

overall throughput   The combination of processor performance, data transfer, and memory access.

packets   Segments of transmitted information.

protocol   A set of rules that govern communication between computers.

simple network management   The protocol that the network management stations and various network devices use to exchange information.

uninterruptible power supply (UPS)   System of batteries and circuits that will allow a computer to function during a power outage.

UNIX   Multiuser multitasking operating system from AT&T that runs on a wide variety of computer systems, including micros and mainframes.

Chapter 5

Standards

One of the basic characteristics of networks is that they grow and change. That means that you as a LAN user will observe and participate in these changes. Fortunately, there are movements within the computer industry to minimize the problems caused by the chaos of endless flux. The movement toward standards pervades the industry. Ultimately, network standards exist to keep change from becoming disruption. Standards let computer systems change how they do things without changing what they do.

This chapter illuminates some of the areas where standards are still evolving.

Protocols and Standards

The idea of standards is not new to just about anyone who has ever tried to share files with someone who uses a different application program. Let's say that you and a colleague in the same office use identical 486 PCs for word processing but have selected different programs. You use WordPerfect 5.1, and your friend uses Geoworks Geowrite. As long as there is no interaction between the two types of files, there are no compatibility problems. However, when you want to edit a file created by the Geoworks Geowrite user, problems arise. If you try to edit WordPerfect 5.1 files with Geoworks Geowrite you could end up with strange characters, format errors, and lots of dumb looks on your face.

These problems arise because the two programs use proprietary, incompatible file formats. Each program uses different codes to indicate special features, such as italicized type or special information such as a file's beginning, end, size, and other characteristics. Your program, however, won't recognize another program's codes and vice versa.

In short, each application program maintains unique standards within its own domain. However, in the real world, not everyone shares the same taste in programs. You have two basic options if you want to share information from different applications. You can share files created under different programs if you:

- use file-conversion software, or
- import files in ASCII format.

ASCII

ASCII, pronounced *ask-key*, stands for American Standard Code for Information Interchange. Also known as text format or DOS format, ASCII is a prime example of an industry standard. When a document is saved as an ASCII file, most special formatting belonging to proprietary programs is lost. However, all text is preserved.

Protocols

With LANs, we talk about protocols almost as much as we talk about standards. You may already be familiar with the term *protocol* as it is used in diplomatic circles to cover specialized customs. The term has a similar meaning in the computer world. A network operating system must support a variety of computers. It must "learn" the customs and languages of these systems.

A protocol, then, is a set of rules. A communications protocol defines rules for:

- setting up a communications connection
- terminating a communications connection
- beginning a transaction
- ending a transaction
- formatting the communicated information
- controlling access to communications facilities

There are dozens of protocols now used with computers and communications networks. *TCP/IP* is currently the most widely used protocol on earth. It is the standard for the Internet.

Protocol Organizations

Who sets up these protocols? In the diplomatic world, sometimes large international agencies such as the United Nations make rules of conduct. The computer world also has its organizational bodies, known as *standards bodies*. These include the International Standards Organization (ISO), the National Institute for Standards and Technology (NIST), formerly the National Bureau of Standards (NBS), and the Association for Information and Image Management (AIIM), which sets standards for any products related to electronic imaging. The Department of Defense has set up its own set of protocols known as the Transmission Control Protocol/Internet Protocol (TCP/IP), which is also used by many other federal agencies.

On the other hand, in the world of diplomacy, sometimes powerful nations set up their own systems of protocol. This also happens in the computer world. Sometimes a manufacturer of a computing system or LAN will design an original proprietary communications protocol. For example, most of IBM's larger computer systems depend on a coordinated set of protocols known as Systems Network Architecture (SNA). IBM has also begun implementing Systems Applications Architecture (SAA).

When an influential manufacturer, such as Hewlett-Packard, Apple Computer, or IBM initiates the protocol, other manufacturers may follow suit. In other words, with sufficient support from other vendors and users, a proprietary protocol can become a de facto standard for the entire industry.

GOVERNING GROUP STANDARDS

However, standards endorsed by governing groups are often accepted as "more standard" than de facto standards created by manufacturers. Born of consensus, standards endorsed by governing groups are not tainted by an individual company's priorities. Even so, computer industry standards are always in flux. New standards are constantly emerging and old ones struggle to survive.

One of the most important protocols in a LAN is the one that determines how information is broadcast. The two protocols most often used in LANs are the *carrier-sense, multiple-access collision-detection* (CSMA/CD) and the token-ring access methods. CSMA/CD is also known as a statistical access method, while token-ring access is also known as a deterministic method.

USER INTERFACE STANDARDS

Standards are bringing consistency to the way your programs look and feel. The advantage of a common *graphical user interface* (GUI) is that you can use similar commands to do similar things in different programs. For example, every program lets you decide how much of the screen its display should take up in the same way. A GUI can eliminate the need to master completely different sets of basic commands for each application.

GUI standards are closely related to operating systems. The UNIX community is still trying to agree on a standard GUI. DOS environments also lack a standard GUI. Windows is popular and Microsoft has gone as far as making a network that features Windows: Windows for Workgroups. However, one key drawback of Windows is that it does not work on older, less powerful DOS-based computers. Quarterdeck's DESQview is also popular with DOS machines. Meanwhile, IBM promotes Presentation Manager as the GUI of choice for OS/2 systems.

PRINTER STANDARDS

Printers are another arena raising the question of standards. Printers need standards so that every piece of software doesn't have to know how to communicate with each of the thousands of different printers on the market. Over the years, one of the biggest debates has concerned compatibility with PostScript, the page description language developed by Adobe Systems and considered a standard in the Macintosh world. Originally, *PostScript* was held up as the highest standard for printers. However, many consultants now agree that non-PostScript printers are usually better for text, and they are less expensive as well. Hewlett-Packard's PCL language has become a rival standard for printer control languages.

FIBER-OPTIC STANDARDS

The rising popularity of fiber optics is based on its speed. A modern PC can read 200 typewritten pages of text from its disk each second, but old-fashioned 10-Mbps Ethernet can typically transmit at only half that speed. LANs can be slow.

While 100-Mbps Ethernet over traditional wiring is becoming more popular, another key method for increasing network speed is to install *Fiber Distributed Data Interface* (FDDI), the high-speed 100-Mbps (megabits per second) fiber-optic network developed by the American National Standards Institute (ANSI).

FDDI technology is expensive. It can cost almost twice as much as copper-based technologies, such as Ethernet and Token-Ring. Another traditional drawback has been that while FDDI supplies high-speed backbones, it has lacked high-speed connections to the desktop for engineering and image applications. But this is changing. This is of particular concern to users with engineering or image applications who need to connect high-speed networks to the desktop. That is why various groups have been examining ways of achieving FDDI speeds with copper wiring, shielded twisted-pair cabling, and unshielded twisted pair.

Synchronous Optical Network (SONET) is another fiber-optic standard. SONET governs high-speed transmission over fiber-optic cable. It is most relevant to telephone companies and anyone else building very large networks.

Asynchronous Transfer Mode (ATM)

Asynchronous transfer mode (ATM) is a high-speed data transmission technology available for both local and wide area networks. AT&T and US Sprint are using ATM over a wide area and are offering multi-megabit data transmission services to customers. Eventually, it will be used for in-house networks. (However, for now, fast Ethernet technologies and switching hubs are considered preferable and most cost-effective.) ATM supports many types of traffic, including voice, data, facsimile, real-time video, imaging, and CD-quality audio. It can be used with many topologies.

ATM takes advantage of the high data throughput rate offered by fiber-optic cables. High-speed ATM implementations (155 to 622 Mbps) use the Synchronous Optical Network (SONET). ATM is also considered appropriate for private networks that include desktop personal computers. Many analysts see 155-Mbps ATM boards becoming popular in personal computers by the end of the decade.

T I P

ATM makes network management easier when it is used as a corporate backbone. This is because ATM eliminates many problems caused by complex internetworks with different addressing schemes and routing mechanisms. ATM hubs provide connections between any two ports on the hub. The addresses of the attached devices are premapped; this makes it easy to send messages from one node to another. The best way to phase in ATM within an organization is to use a hierarchical distributed wiring structure. In a multistory office building you would first install a main ATM switch as a backbone that links the connections from floor to floor. Next you would install ATM switches on each floor to connect high-performance servers installed there. When the cost of ATM boards goes down, you could connect user systems directly to the ATM switches.

For more information about ATM contact the ATM Forum at (415) 926-2585.

Multivendor Network Standards

If only one vendor made all of the systems today, you wouldn't have to worry about these standards. The reality, of course, is that there are numerous vendors. That in turn creates a need for standards, facilitating the integration of multivendor networks. Chapter 6, which covers the major vendors and their offerings, explains the positioning of some of these standards in more detail.

The best-known true standards for internetwork communications are the transmission control protocol (TCP) and Internet protocol (IP), together known as TCP/IP. The United States government, the first and largest user of multivendor networks, has spurred development of TCP/IP for more than 20 years. TCP/IP is also viewed as the most efficient path toward compliance with OSI (open systems interconnect), an internationally promoted network scheme. OSI's goal is to promote truly interoperable systems. (For more information on TCP/IP, see Chapter 12.)

Network Management Standards

Many of the vendors supporting TCP/IP have also endorsed *SNMP* (simple network management protocol). SNMP is a standard method for passing network management information among diverse products. Meanwhile, three other protocols are gaining popularity:

- Common management information services (CMIS)
- Common management information protocol (CMIP)
- Common management over TCP/IP (CMOT)

The movement has been toward these newer protocols. CMOT has been promoted as an interim step between SNMP and full compliance with CMIP and CMIS. Many vendors, however, have moved directly from SNMP to CMIP and CMIS. No one predicts, however, that SNMP will go away. Most leading vendors will offer extensive support of SNMP, CMIP, and CMIS. No network vendor with long-term vision can afford to ignore these protocols.

SNMP is rapidly growing on smaller networks as manageable hubs grow in popularity.

T I P

Electronic File Exchange Standards

Electronic mail (E-mail) is also being standardized. The primary E-mail standards are X.400, X.500, and MHS (Message Handling Service). E-mail standards address the problem of quickly finding where to send a message to someone halfway across the world.

The standards X.400 and X.500 are being developed by the Consultative Committee on International Telephony and Telegraphy (CCITT). Novell, on the other hand, is promoting MHS.

X.400

Many industry analysts say that X.400 will do for E-mail what the CCITT Group 3 and 4 standards did for faxes. The purpose of X.400 is to cross the barriers created by proprietary protocols found in most E-mail systems. In other words, compliance with X.400 allows easy interconnection of private and public E-mail systems. The X.400 system works as follows:

1. An E-mail message is sent over a LAN to a PC equipped with a message transfer agent, which is a type of software.

2. The message is converted to a standard format prescribed by the X.400 protocol.

3. The message is transmitted to the addressee.

4. Message agent software converts the message from X.400 format to one that is compatible with the addressee's E-mail.

X.400 is currently being used by:

- IBM PROFS
- Digital Equipment's All-IN-1
- MCI Mail
- AT&T Mail

X.500

The goal of X.500 is to allow E-mail users to look up E-mail addresses on all forms of networks all over the world. Otherwise, networks are limited to directory services for systems identical to the sender.

MESSAGE HANDLING SERVICE (MHS)

Because Novell includes MHS as part of its NetWare product, MHS has become a de facto E-mail standard. In general, MHS works in much the same way as X.400. A PC on the LAN acts as an MHS intermediary and transfers messages between networks when the receiver and the sender are incompatible.

The OSI Model

With all the different types of standards for network hardware and software, wouldn't it be nice if there was a framework for discussing them? Fortunately, this framework exists. The OSI model consists of seven layers that define which part of the network communications problem a given piece of software should focus on. The layers are:

- **Physical.** This layer covers cabling standards so users know what kind of wire to buy.

- **Data Link.** The data link layer concerns itself with packaging data into data frames—packets containing data and control information. This lets users predict which NICs can be used together.

- **Network.** Concerned with packet switching, this layer establishes virtual circuits between computers or terminals for data communication. This lets NIC manufacturers know how to control data package exchanges with other vendor's equipment.

- **Transport.** This level covers error recognition and recovery as well as the multiplexing of messages and the regulating of information flow. This gives network operating systems a safe way to pass data packets between workstations.

- **Session.** This is the level handling password recognition, logon and logoff procedures, network monitoring and reporting, and all network management functions. This describes what kind of passwords and signals can be used to allow sharing data between users.

- **Presentation**. This level covers files transfers, network security, and format functions. Adherence to such standards, for example, lets Macs and PCs exchange data files.

- **Application**. Electronic mail, database managers, file server software, and printer server software are at this level, which handles messages, remote logons, and the responsibility for network management statistics. Adhering to these standards lets all programs talk over the network in the same way.

Putting It All Together

You can find standards in all phases of the LAN industry. Many of these standards are still evolving. If you are not careful, you could end up with a LAN product that is out of date. Remember beta video cassettes and 8-track tapes? The computer field is also littered with the remains of products that are no longer suited to current market conditions. Still, your emphasis as a consumer should always be on finding the best solutions for your situation.

Glossary

ASCII	A binary code for data in communications, most minicomputers and all personal computers.
asynchronous transfer mode (ATM)	A high-speed data transfer technology used on both local and wide area networks.
FDDI	Fiber Distributed Data Interface, the high-speed 100 Mbps (megabits per second) fiber-optic network the American National Standards Institute (ANSI) has developed.
fiber distributed data interface(FDDI)	The high speed 100 mbps fiber-optic network developed by the American National standards Institute.

graphical user interface (GUI)	The use of icons in place of typed commands as a way of commanding a computer.
message handling service MHS	A Novell E-mail service.
PCL	Page Control Language, a page description language developed by Hewlett Packard.
PostScript	Adobe Systems–developed page description language for printers.
Standards bodies	Groups of industry professionals who determine the methods that will be used throughout the industry, as in creating communications protocols.
synchronous optical network (SONET)	A fiber optic network standard.
TCP/IP	The most widely used protocol on earth. It is the standard for the Internet.
transmission control protocol/internet protocol (TCP/IP)	A data communications protocol.
X.400	An E-mail standard designed to connect public and private systems.
X.500	An E-mail standard designed to allow users to look up E-mail addresses.

Chapter 6

Selected LAN Vendors and Their Offerings

The interest in LANs is growing rapidly. According to International Data Corporation (IDC), the dollar value of PC LAN operating systems shipped rose 54% from 1989 to 1990 to $1.14 billion, and is expected to grow to more than $2.8 billion during 1995. IDC's "1991 Analysis of the PC LAN Operating System Market" also predicts worldwide LAN license shipments will increase from 400,000 in 1990 to 610,000 in 1995, and the number of PCs connected by LANs will swell from 16 million in 1990 to 60 million during 1995.

Some analysts, however, point out that even these robust figures could be better. They argue that LAN growth is slowed by the lack of tools to keep track of what's happening on bigger LANs. They point out that connecting LANs with one another is difficult. Network software developers, in turn, are burdened with writing separate versions of software for:

- Novell Inc.'s NetWare
- Microsoft Corp.'s NT Server
- Banyan Systems Inc.'s VINES
- DOS-based peer-to-peer NETBIOS LANs like LANtastic and PowerLAN.
- OS/2 LAN server
- Windows for workgroups

While these giants work out their differences, the best thing we can hope for is to understand the most popular systems, get to understand their strengths and weaknesses, and pick the ones that work best for us. For example, basic LANs are best used only for small workgroups or businesses; others accommodate larger organizations.

Mixed Platform Support

The world of LANs changes very quickly. Individual vendors are constantly tweaking their products. While certain "oldies but goodies" are not likely to make a comeback, many times companies are reluctant to get rid of a system they like just because it is no longer a significant player. Yes, there are probably even a very small number of 3-Com systems operating out there. However, older, obsolete systems tend to fall by the wayside as the field evolves. Today's market is dominated by IBM, Microsoft, Novell, and various UNIX vendors. Some operating systems are gravitating towards the client. Others, such as Windows, are gravitating towards the server. Some, such as Windows NT 3.5, are gravitating toward both.

Overall LAN Hardware Differences

Believe it or not, the hardware differences among LANs are less pronounced than the software differences. With most basic LANs, for example, any workstation can also be a server. Most advanced system manufacturers discourage the use of nondedicated workstations as servers.

There are some differences between basic systems and more advanced server systems. Installation differences are key. The average LAN manager or user probably could install a zero-slot system. After all, you usually don't have to open the basic computer box during the installation. Instead, you need only attach wires and install software.

Most networks, on the other hand, require the installation of network interface cards. Users with advanced repair skills might be able to attempt these installations. However, it is still a good idea to use professional installers. In many cases, technical support staffs at computer stores can handle the job. However, most advanced LAN systems are better installed by professional installers, including experienced LAN resellers.

Cost Differences

The most obvious and sometimes most easily understood difference between systems is cost. Managers these days are particularly cost-conscious. The harsh reality, however, is that high network costs can limit network availability, growth, and enhancement.

Cost differences sometimes are difficult to assess. Vendors of the most advanced systems sometimes avoid disclosing prices. Others allow potential users to bring up the cost-per-node costs.

Cost-per-node reflects the cost of connecting each user's workstation. This amount usually includes the cost of:

- The workstation's network interface adapter
- The connecting cable
- A share of the cost of the required network software
- Adjusting existing circuit cards to allow for the addition of the NIC without conflict

As a general rule, the per-node cost of a basic LAN usually is under $500. On the other hand, the per-node cost of an advanced LAN can exceed $1,000. Nevertheless, cost-per-node is really only a starting point. Costs can also climb because every LAN installation has unique requirements, such as applications to be supported or the type of cabling to be used. That is why many vendors quote prices for total systems, including hardware and software, that are designed for a fixed number of users.

NetWare

Three out of four PC LANs use Novell NetWare. Novell encourages versatility by developing new products to meet the changes in the marketplace. For example, when 386 computers became state-of-the-art, Novell developed NetWare 386. Novell also developed NetWare Lite to compete with other peer-to-peer systems. The rise of NetWare's popularity has also spawned the birth of Portable NetWare, a kernal product aimed at the UNIX and VAX markets.

The Netware Family

Novell offers a variety of network operating systems under the name NetWare. These range from the simple and inexpensive NetWare Lite to NetWare 4.X, an operating system designed for complex enterprise systems. As of this writing, NetWare accounted for three million users and a 70% market share. The full product lines include:

- NetWare Lite
- NetWare 3.x
- NetWare 4.x

NETWARE LITE

This peer-to-peer network operating system is designed for between two and 25 users. It runs on top of the DOS operating system and is compatible with Windows. Users set up a network for sharing files, applications, and printers.

NETWARE 3.X AND 4.X

Both NetWare 3.x and 4.x are network operating systems designed to support hundreds of users on a single, dedicated server. They can integrate diverse systems, including minicomputers. NetWare 4.x inherits all the capabilities of NetWare 3.x and adds features of its own. These features create a multiserver environment providing directory services and enterprise network support. People who jump from 3.x to 4.x notice key differences; the object-oriented design of 4.x is very foreign to 3.0 users.

NetWare introduced a network structure known as NetWare Directory Services in Version 4.0. Widely acknowledged to be a potentially powerful and sophisticated way of administering large networks, NDS lacked a crucial feature—the capacity to make significant changes in the directory structure once it had been defined. Version 4.1, however, corrected that problem. A NetWare 4.1 server can administer as many as 12 NetWare 3.x servers by adding them to the NDS context.

T I P

Although Novell promotes the NDS database as a selling feature, you can partition it and make replicas on other servers. If a server goes down, users on that server can still log into the network by using a replica.

NetWare 4.1 also includes an integrated system, Storage Management Services (SMS), to back up files across the network on both servers and workstations. SMS will back up any workstation file independent of client operating systems. It also includes the NetWare Message Handling Services (NMHS) as part of the operating software. It comes with a simple E-mail package knows as First Mail as well, and includes facilities for enhanced internetwork routing.

Why NetWare is Popular

NetWare has many advantages, including a wide user base. This widespread acceptance carries with it advantages such as consumer familiarity and broad popular support. Many supporters see NetWare as the de facto standard for LANs. NetWare accommodates many types of systems, including UNIX.

Speed is another advantage. The proprietary software built into the network operating system manages files and directories on the hard disk, creating a fast file system. Also, the large installed base has given rise to a large number of follow-on software and hardware products designed specifically for use with Novell's software. It also offers good security, robustness and broad applications support.

NetWare Drawbacks

NetWare does have its drawbacks, however. Critics have problems with the proprietary file system, which speeds up performance but can be difficult to work with. DOS utilities, such as Norton's Disk Utilities, will not work on a NetWare server. Novell's emphasis on software at the expense of new hardware development has been criticized.

VINES: A UNIX Solution

Banyan Systems designed Visual Networking System (VINES) to support both PC-to-PC communications and links with other non-DOS operating systems. VINES is based primarily upon the UNIX operating system, which was designed to support multitasking and access to a wide variety of resources for multiple users. In addition to UNIX systems, VINES has the ability (like all other major players) to support:

- DOS workstations
- OS/2-based workstations
- Macintosh workstations
- Popular minicomputers

One of the key strengths of VINES is easy expandability. A VINES LAN can start with a few users, then grow into a very large network—without replacing the network operating system. Another key strength is the StreetTalk global naming service, which allows assignment of logical, easily remembered or located names to network users and resources. Although many users are intimidated by the idea of a UNIX system, VINES has a menu-driven user-interface. In February 1995, Banyan had an 8% market share. However, it is a favorite of large systems. VINES accounts for half of all enterprise users with over 50 users connected to a single server.

AppleTalk

AppleTalk is a set of specifications describing how to connect Apple Macintosh computers, printers, and other resources into a communications network. Networking with the Macintosh is extremely simple because networking functions are directly built in. It now supports both Token Ring and Ethernet technologies.

Traditionally, AppleTalk has been thought of as better for low-traffic use than for large, business-wide enterprise networks. There have been criticisms based on cross-platform standardization problems, and some reviewers have said that the product is clunky and slow. However, this seems to be changing. Continued development has led to some broader, more ambitious applications of AppleTalk. For example, the Lexington, MA Public School District now links its NetWare and AppleTalk Ethernet LANs over existing cable TV lines.

LANtastic

LANtastic operates at a speed of 2 and 10 megabits per second on 10BaseT and 10Base2 media. This rate does not match the 4- to 16-megabit speeds of most advanced LANs. However, most people find the speed acceptable. LANtastic's strong suits are ease of installation, flexibility and price. The cost can be under $250 per connected PC, including the network operating system, interface cards, cables, and terminators. Artisoft has added many enhancements to LANtastic over the years, including support for CD-ROM drives and telephone dial-in connections.

PCs are logged into the LAN via NET, a menu-driven program. Commands for logging onto the network can also be included in the DOS-based AUTOEXEC.BAT file, which is run automatically whenever a PC is started. Once the network software is launched, the user has immediate access to all authorized features, including E-mail and print spooling. (A print spooler is software that creates a buffer where data files to be printed can be stored while they wait their turn.)

LANtastic also supports OS/2 now. Artisoft's LANtastic for OS/2 network operating system offers 32-bit multitasking abilities. It does not, however, include the programs for scheduling and E-mail found LANtastic 6.0 for Windows.

LANtastic uses network interface cards for most types of IBM compatibles. If you buy Artisoft NICs, they offer coaxial cable and twisted pair adapters for under $300.

LANtastic for NetWare

For those of you who have trouble deciding whether to use NetWare or LANtastic, the good news is that your network can use both. Artisoft makes LANtastic for NetWare to let you set up a peer-to-peer workgroup within your existing Novell LAN. The LANtastic software runs transparently with NetWare so workstations can share printers, drives, and other resources placed anywhere on the network, and still retain access to NetWare services. You can share such specialized devices as tape backups, CD-ROM, or WORM drives. Workstations can share files and printers directly without going through the NetWare server, enabling you to locate your resources around the network and reduce the NetWare server's workload. NetWare users on LANtastic-equipped segments can also take advantage of LANtastic disk caching, sound capability and highly flexible security.

LANtastic for NetWare software uses less than 20K in a LANtastic workstation and less than 60K in a LANtastic peer server (not including NetBIOS and ODI drivers). You can load the LANtastic system into high memory, leaving conventional memory for application software.

Other reasons for using LANtastic for NetWare include:

- The LANtastic for NetWare system provides a legitimate means of adding more users on the network beyond the NetWare-specified limits. The LANtastic portion of the system allows up to 500 users.

- LANtastic for NetWare offers flexible print job scheduling. You can request immediate despooling, so a large job begins printing before the file finishes spooling to the print server's hard drive which can be located at any convenient network station. Alternately, you can request "delayed despooling" which lets you specify a time to run print jobs. You can schedule a long print job for such non-peak times as evenings and weekends.

- LANtastic software also serves as a safety net, allowing users to continue working on the LANtastic segment of the system in the event a NetWare server goes down or off-line.

ARCnet

ARCnet (Attached Resource Computer Network), developed as far back as 1977, is a reliable, low-cost token bus cabling system that provides a physical star and a logical ring. It uses a character-oriented protocol. Standard ARCnet is capable of transmitting data at a speed of 2.5 Mbs, while a new version provides 20 Mbs. Some consultants avoid this product, however, because it uses a media access approach that is non-IEEE standard. Its supporters, however, consider it a de facto standard.

10Net

Tiara has developed a family of alternative LAN products over the years. They have a reputation for low-cost solutions and strong security features. The product can be configured to form a 1-Mbs bus network topology or a star architecture.

Communications is one of 10Net's strengths. 10Net offers CHAT, a program allowing brief conversations between users. It also comes with Network Courier, a leading electronic mail product. In addition, a feature known as CB permits users to have public discussion forums. There is also a built-in bulletin board program.

A node that shares its resources under 10Net is called a *superstation*. 10Net uses the NET SHARE command to share resources. It also uses the NET USE command to use a particular resource. Like LANtastic, the NET commands are inherited from the IBM PC network program. It is now available for NetWare.

Microsoft And IBM

IBM and Microsoft have taken care to design serious network products. They provide speedy file and print services and symmetric multiprocessing support (SMP), which enables the operating system to distribute its processing load among all available processors, keeping them equally busy. They also offer virtual memory.

NT Server

NT Advanced Server is a LAN operating system from Microsoft that runs as an application under WIndows in a server and supports DOS, OS/2 and UNIX workstations. It uses the Microsoft File Sharing protocol (SMB) for file sharing and the NETBIOS protocol for its transport mechanism. Today, many of the networking features of NT Server are migrating to Windows NT. It is being promoted as an alternative to NetWare as an application server, and a file and print server. NT Server is also recognized as a multi-tasking database server with a full complement of development tools. Likewise, NT workstation is considered a powerful competitor to UNIX workstation programs.

There are now over 1200 applications for both the workstation and the server, as compared to only 200 as of 1994. The pace of development for Windows NT is obviously quite rapid.

IBM's LAN Server

IBM has had mixed success in the network field. However, it may be gaining ground now. At the time of the writing of this book, IBM Server 4.0 had a 10% market share. IBM also has a software package designed to be used by OS/2 systems. IBM's OS/2 Server 4.0 Advanced is considered a great improvement over previous versions. IBM is struggling to reestablish itself with its new versions of OS/2. Users have generally shied away from OS/2 because of poor implementation of earlier versions. The most recent version of OS/2 Warp (version 3) is widely regarded as greatly improved over previous versions, and offers true multi-tasking and multithreading, along with a renewed commitment on IBM's behalf toward the product. It takes advantage of OS/2s object-oriented capabilities to provide a strong new set of graphical administration tools.

T I P

LAN Server can access up to 4 gigabytes of memory. It requires 13 megabytes of RAM.

Windows for Workgroups

Of particular interest to LAN users is the recent development of Windows for Workgroups. This system combines the familiar Windows operating version 3.1 with easy-to-use networking. In fact, Microsoft offers a Windows for Workgroups User Kit that includes both hardware and software. You can also use Windows for Workgroups to connect to an NT Advanced Server or to Novell NetWare.

This peer-to-peer system lets you E-mail associates, schedule group meetings, share files and printers, manage calendars, and work together on group projects. Group projects are enhanced by the network's Dynamic Data Exchange (DDE) which allows you to insert information into your document from documents owned by other users, even if those documents reside on other network computers. It is compatible with Windows NT and Novell NetWare, as well as with Banyan VINES.

WARNING

Windows for Workgroups has limited security features. Microsoft Windows NT or Novell NetWare is recommended for people who have high security needs.

Windows NT

The newest generation of Windows is Windows NT, a 32-bit operating system. It runs on 386 (and higher) computers. It also includes built-in networking and advanced security features. Many people believe that a Windows NT Server is more streamlined than a NetWare server. A Windows NT server finds the user information it needs only when it needs it, eliminating the need to constantly move unnecessary information. Windows NT is also noted for its automatic hardware detection capabilities.

T I P

Windows NT has largely replaced another Microsoft product, LAN Manager, a network management and file system that runs on top of the OS/2 operating system.

NOTE While Windows NT is easier to administer than UNIX and includes many attractive features, it is a young program. It does have security options and significant horsepower, which has impressed critics. It also has significant TCP/IP capabilities. However, it is still lacks the number of server packages, development tools and utilities that can be found for UNIX.

Putting It All Together

All LANs are not created equal, nor should they be. Some LANs are designed for small work groups or businesses. Other basic LANs are designed for more complex situations. Differences also exist in cost (a difficult factor to determine), cabling requirements, and software applications supported. While some consultants suggest it is best to stay with the handful of best-known and most popular vendors, everyone agrees that you should investigate all choices thoroughly before making a purchase.

Always remember to plan for growth. The most common mistake network planners make is underestimating their growth needs.

Glossary

Banyan VINES

A network operating system based on UNIX, supports a wide variety of hardware platforms, and requires a dedicated file server. VINES stands for Virtual Networking System.

Dynamic Data Exchange (DDE)

A Windows for Workgroups facility that allows you to insert information in your document from documents owned by other users, even if those documents reside on other network computers.

First Mail

A simple E-mail package included with NetWare 4.1.

Netware Message Handling Services (NMHS)

An integrated system included with Net-Ware 4.1. It includes facilities for enhanced internetwork routing.

print spooler

Software that allows printing to take place in the background while other tasks are performed in the foreground.

Storage Management Services (SMS)

An integrated system included with NetWare 4.1 to back up files across the network on both servers and workstations. SMS will back up any workstation file independent of client operating systems.

Superstation

A node that shares its resources under 10Net is called a superstation. 10Net uses the NET SHARE command to show resources. It also uses the NET USE command to use a particular resource.

symmetric multiprocessing support (SMP)

A method of boosting system performance by offloading operating chores from the primary processor to additional processors.

Chapter 7

Maintaining Your LAN

You can be sure that maintaining a network involves much more than dusting off the cables. The ease of installation and usability of distributed systems may have created a myth that these dispersed systems do not need management. Actually, they need innovative management techniques to deal with distributed responsibilities. In addition to network administrators, individual users need to get involved to ensure networks are well-maintained and reliable.

The Importance of Maintenance

You may have already heard of client/server computing, and expect to hear more about it in this book and in the outside world. Today, running and maintaining a system involves developing clear ideas about what information needs sharing and how to share it before you commit your-selves to any particular LAN. Connections alone don't guarantee easy access or LAN success.

The keys to LAN maintenance are:

- Start with PCs in good condition on a LAN that is functioning perfectly, with a written record of how each PC is configured

- A backup policy that covers every user of the network, requiring no more than a few minutes of simple procedures per day per user, one or two people should be responsible for verifying sys-tem-wide backups

- Virus checking of all new software before sharing it among users

- Limiting responsibility for file server condition to a small number of people

- Checking a LAN's electrical integrity yearly, and after adding or dropping users

Backing Up Your Files

The only way you can really protect your computer work fully is to make duplicate copies, known as *backups*. That way if your computer is dam-aged or stolen, or if you erase data accidentally, the backup is available as a substitute. In other words, you should think of backups as an insurance policy—hopefully, you won't need them, but if you do, they are there. You should consider keeping your backup disks at a remote location away from your computer. Assume, for example, a manufacturer puts its shipment billing information on the computer in an office that falls vic-tim to a fire. If the backup disks and the computer are in the same room, both could be destroyed.

You can backup files from individual workstations; you do not need a LAN to do backups. Backups are easy to do and do not take much time, rarely more than 15 minutes per day. You should make backups as often as possible. That way, should you run into a problem your losses will be minimal. If you make backups every day you will only lose one day's work should something go wrong.

File Server Backups

One of the key reasons people turn to LANs is for their backup capacities. LAN file servers can have their own backup systems. For example, Palindrome Corporation's version 2.0d and later of its Network Archivist backup system for NetWare LANs runs on the network server. (It can also run on a separate LAN workstation that needs to be dedicated to backup only when archival is occurring.) It is largely automated. An unattended restore function lets the system restore lost files without administrator intervention, unless tapes need to be changed.

Three Steps Toward LAN Management

Whatever you do, do not fall for the myth that because distributed systems are easy to install and use they don't need to be managed. The fact is that every system sharing resources among multiple users requires management. The type of management, however, is changing. In the past, most information service management consisted of placing several professionals in charge of a single computer. Today, however, you have distributed management, where individual professionals manage multiple computers in distributed environments.

Step 1: Risk Analysis

What will happen if one part of your system fails? Risk analysis answers this question. Risk analysis will also help you determine the need for *fault tolerance*, the name given to the taking over and continuing of normal operations in the event of a primary component failure. In some cases, you will want to make sure you have plenty of backups, such as spare memory cards, disk drives, cables, or workstations. In other cases, risk analysis will point out where fault tolerance is not a cost-effective and reliable strategy.

Intelligent power protection should also be planned. You should have battery backup power for critical workstations. Every way possible, you need to avoid the problems associated with brownouts and blackouts. Battery units cost around $120 per computer at discount computer stores.

Step 2: Data Disaster Recovery Planning

Nobody likes the idea of thinking about disasters, but they do happen. While you can't plan them away, you can minimize their impact. Your plan should include both backup and off-site storage. Backup copies of all applications programs, in both their original and user-configured versions, need to be stored off site. Backups should be performed daily. You will also need to develop procedures for testing the verification of backup data.

Larger systems may benefit from the use of disaster recovery services, such as Comdisco and Sungard. These services will develop disaster plans and manage off-site storage.

TIP

Step 3: System Management

Systems management requires three elements:

- reliable hardware
- reliable software
- reliable administrator(s)

Besides reliable hardware components, systems need software utilities to manage the hardware. These utilities are easy-to-use software tools for system management making local management easier and a prerequisite for remote management. Some software utilities, such as the virus scanners mentioned previously, monitor system health, then provide warnings that help managers locate problems quickly.

TIP IBM and Hewlett Packard are among the companies selling Simple Network Management Protocol (SNMP)-based management software that allows detailed network monitoring (including port and card level) and control.

Every reliable system should have a system administrator. How much training this person needs will depend upon the requirements of your system. Obviously, if your system is large and complex you will need to have an administrator with more training than a zero slot LAN would require.

Administrators, in larger systems especially, will need extra help from LAN management software. The cost of placing an administrator on every LAN subnetwork would be prohibitive. Many of the more dispersed systems, such as MANs and WANs, also require remote management using hardware and software tools.

Monitors and Analyzers

Large networks often use sophisticated maintenance tools, including monitors, network probes and analyzers. These tools evaluate network transmissions.

The ideal network management solution, consultants say, is a mix of monitoring and analysis. A proper mix of monitoring and analysis provides the near optimum combination of trend analysis, fault identification, and troubleshooting. Monitors allow you to watch the network constantly while analyzers let you clear faults as they occur.

Monitors

A monitor is a hardware/software unit that offers limited insights. It can, for example, report excessive collisions on Ethernet. However, it cannot tell you the reason for the collisions. It can't even give insight to the possible causes. A monitor can tell you that the network is slowing down, but it can't tell you with any certainty what is causing the slowdown. It can tell you that a network segment is down. A few of the more sophisticated monitors, such as Cabletron's Spectrum, can tell you where the actual discontinuity is likely to be.

Probes

A probe differs from a monitor only in that probes are usually placed on the network segments and report their results to a central point. Monitors, on the other hand, are self-contained.

Analyzers

Analyzers observe at all levels the activity within the packets passing on the network and decode those packets for technicians to see. The analyzer, unlike the monitor, looks inside the data packet to reveal the cause of a problem. Analyzers can decode packet contents and display them in English or hexadecimal. In addition to studying the packets of information flowing across a network, an analyzer can provide valuable statistics, covering the performance of the network's software, file server, and interface card. Because of the vast amount of information passing through a protocol analyzer, users filter it by establishing parameters. The user, for example, may analyze station address, protocol, or particular frame patterns. Ironically, sophisticated network probes, which require agents on the network segment being monitored to work, are often far more expensive than analyzers. Most sophisticated probe systems are highly graphical.

Using protocol analyzers, for all of their benefits, has one drawback for most organizations: education. The technicians and administrators who use them must be well-schooled in network architecture and protocols. In short, if your administrators are not well trained, an analyzer with a five-figure price tag will do you little good. Fortunately, with some practice a network manager can read analyzer reports with relative ease.

Network Documentation

Documentation is an industry term for the instructions supplied with computer hardware and software. Many consultants recommend the creation of personal network documentation above and beyond the instruction manuals that come with your PCs and linking equipment. The first step in creating appropriate documentation is to identify the tasks specific to your personal day-to-day agenda. This document should be as brief as possible, containing only the steps need to get you started on your tasks, such as:

- logging on the network
- backing up file
- turning everything off

In the beginning, you will focus on the simplest tasks. Eventually, however, you will want to develop personal guides that walk you through individual tasks, such as writing and distributing a one-page memo or using E-mail. As you can see, some of these tasks require using several different components. The idea is to have instructions available where you need them the most.

You should then test your LAN "cheat sheets" by running through all the steps. (You should, of course, avoid disclosing passwords or any other information that could breach security.) Also, you be sure to date your personal documentation. After all, you will want to update your instructions after you update your LAN.

You can, of course, still use the documentation that comes with your system components. However, most documentation for LAN products offers little, if any guidance about product interoperability. Observers have noted that this absence is particularly frustrating to users because LAN products are meant to be connected with other products. Even documentation that is complete can be a mixed blessing. Often manuals focus on product features instead of describing the steps needed to complete specific tasks. In other words, typical word processing documentation will cover subjects such as "Using Macros," which is great if you know what a macro is and want to use one, but rarely cover how-to's such as "What To Do To Create A One Page Letter."

Often documentation is just useless. It makes sense only to those who already understand what they are doing. Many LAN users, like many PC users, have their own documentation horror stories. Because LANs are more complex than PCs, documentation for LAN components and applications tends to be more complex than that for independent PCs.

Enterprise Wide Documentation

If you are using more than one computer system, you should consider adding special documentation to cover interactions. You should create a map of all components in your immediate system, including their:

- functions
- capacities
- limitations

You will also want to include general information about other LANs and systems with which you will interact, as well as the types of connections you will use.

Some consultants recommend the creation of a telephone directory listing numbers of people who are useful to LAN management and interconnectivity. This list will cover sources capable of solving emergency problems and providing help. Useful numbers include:

- applications software technical support
- vendors
- service contractors
- network administrators
- MIS personnel

Virus Protection

Unfortunately, viruses are a serious threat to networks, and your particular local area network is susceptible to epidemics. The problem of computer viruses is bad and not getting any better. Six new viruses were discovered every day in 1991, according to the National Computer Security Association. There are now roughly 800 known computer viruses. Some are exclusive to DOS and Mac operating systems, but virus creators are beginning to turn out the first parasites that can exist on both desktop and server operating systems such as NetWare and UNIX.

The first line of defense against viruses is the use of simple security measures. For example, you shouldn't put executable files on the server in directories where users can change them; nor should you leave computers on at night. Those systems that have dial-in access should restrict it through passwords. Companies worried about malicious viruses being implanted by corporate spies or disgruntled former employees, for example, use dial-back modems that not only require remote users to enter their password, but also insist that the caller hang up so the host system then dials them back at a prearranged number.

Minimizing the Virus Threat

The threat of virus attacks to your network can be minimized through proper software and operating practices. For example, a supervisor should never log in from an unchecked workstation. This action could spread a virus from an infected machine to all the places on the network to which you have supervisory rights. Also, you should, whenever possible, segregate executable files into directories that regular users can't overwrite. If a particular program overwrites itself as part of its normal function, you can launch the program from a batch file that first calls a scanner. The batch file should not allow the program to run unless the scanner returns a healthy report.

MIS departments are providing office and home users with courses on virus avoidances and are buying antivirus software. Most viruses enter networks through shared floppy disks. However, the growing popularity of remote access software with LAN connections poses another potential threat. For example, bulletin boards are a point of entry into the LAN. You need to quarantine downloaded files and then check them with a signature scanner before introducing them to your system.

You should also pay careful attention to computers that have been leased or returned recently from an outside repair shop. They may have picked up a virus from another customer; not everyone has high antivirus standards.

What You Can Do

There are an increasing number of defenses against viruses. These include:

- scanners
- memory-resident activity monitors
- software products

There are a number of software scanners that do a good job of detecting viruses. Some scanners have built-in schedulers. Others will work with scheduling utilities. You should check all incoming floppies with a scanner before putting them into network machines. For maximum protection, each workstation should have a:

- Signature scanner, which will identify signatures or previously identified strings of code—known to be viruses—and tell you if you have one, and if you do, exactly which one you have.

- Checksum scanners, which spot unknown viruses. They work on the principle that viruses change the length and content of an executable file by inserting code.

- Memory resident activity monitors, which look for and interrupt viral behavior, such as attempts to format the hard drive.

There is a wide and increasing variety of antivirus software available today. Although some of it is shareware with good reputations, most consultants recommend commercial products. Most of the major antiviral vendors offer periodic (typically quarterly) revisions of their virus signature files. Some offer these updates over their bulletin boards.

Network antivirus software also has to be able to work over remote access. This means having virus protection on communications software. For example, Hilgraeve Inc.'s HyperACCESS (version 5 and above) incorporates a scanning routine that checks a file as it is being downloaded. If it detects a virus signature within the file, it will abort the transfer. Meanwhile, Microcom Inc. has added its Virex antivirus suite to its Carbon Copy Remote Control for the Mac. Any user attempting to transfer a known virus while attached through this software will be unable to do so.

E-Mail Security

Another special security problem for LANs is E-mail. Anyone can send E-mail messages all around the company and many times have the ability to attach files. Price-Waterhouse has developed an anti-virus strategy, writing its own code inside its extensive Lotus Notes system. This software specifically examines E-mail messages with attached files for virus infestation.

Even today, however, most viruses cannot usually infect the core files of common network operating systems, such as NetWare, OS/2-based LAN Manager, or UNIX-based VINES. Still, to be perfectly safe, you can add an antiviral server on the network that checks the network server and attached nodes on a scheduled basis. Some software will also inform your central server of a viral infection. Central Point's Anti-Virus NetWare, for example, can be configured to send a message to the LAN administrator when a virus is detected on an attached PC.

Other Ways to Make Your LAN More Reliable

Every network user can feel personally involved in increasing network reliability. There is no reason why you can't feel personally responsible for your participation in a LAN. You can keep your own inventory of network components with which you interact as well as relevant telephone numbers. Some users go so far as to have technical descriptions of components attached to the devices themselves. In any event, by becoming involved, you increase your personal attention to your work and can help the network administrator and solve emergency problems.

You can also become actively involved in problem resolution and prevention by keeping a problem log. The idea, of course, is to not repeat the same mistakes over and over. A problem log not only documents problems but also allows you to keep records of solutions. A typical log entry for a problem will include appropriate information, such as:

- date
- time
- appropriate circumstances
- response
- effects

Eventually, this log will evolve into a form of personal documentation covering common problems and their solutions. Your network administrator can also combine personal problem logs to identify and solve chronic problems capable of creating network failures and to test vendor claims about product performance and reliability.

Putting It All Together

There is an art and science to maintaining a LAN. Techniques range from the very simple to the very complex. You can use a combination of simple software instructions on an individual PC to backup files, or you can develop an elaborate and centralized backup system. You can use expensive and complicated equipment, such as analyzers, monitors and probes to evaluate transmissions. Meanwhile you should always take care to make sure you have documentation and the telephone numbers of consultants nearby in case problems arise.

Ultimately, as you become more familiar with the network field as a whole you may encounter new philosophical orientations. These philosophical orientations, in turn, impact the way you think about all aspects of network management, including maintenance. Larger systems supporting client/server relationships may require more maintenance than simple peer-to-peer systems. In either case, you may need to work with special LAN management tools. You cannot, however, overlook maintenance at the PC level, including the prevention of viruses.

Glossary

analyzer	Network management tool that studies individual packets.
backups	A set of disks or tapes that contain duplicate copies of your computer files.
client/server computing	Computing done in an environment where individual systems, called servers, support multiple clients, which are users' workstations.

documentation

The instructions supplied with computer hardware and software.

fault tolerance

The name given to the taking over and continuing of normal operations in the event of a primary component.

Graphical User Interface (GUI)

Screen that incorporates icons, pull-down menus, and a mouse, such as those found in Macintosh, Windows, and OS/2 Presentation Manager environments, which controls access to application programs.

monitor

Centralized workstation that assumes responsibility for network management.

probe

Network management tool placed on network segments to be studied, performing a monitor's function.

Simple Network Management Protocol (SNMP)

The most commonly-implemented management environment protocol.

utility

Also known as a desk utility, this is a software program that helps you troubleshoot, repair, and otherwise manage a disk.

Chapter

8

Network Security

Network managers walk a tightrope. They must help users implement and execute security measures. These policies need to be followed rigorously networkwide. They must go beyond the measures that users can implement without interfering with normal work. The best way to maintain this balance is by involving users in the planning and implementation of any security measures. Although the network manager has the ultimate responsibility for security, users also benefit from having their livelihoods and work environments protected.

At the most basic level, managers must implement measures providing as much information as possible about network security and about attempted and successful breaches. Ideally, they should have an ongoing, near-constant audit of network access and use.

Managerial-Level Concerns

This means that LAN managers need to focus on accountability issues. In the long run, this policy can save an organization money. Increasing information about accountability can end up decreasing the liability of any person or group in the face of an accidental or malicious breach of network security.

LAN managers also have the somewhat unexpected problem of tapped lines. LANs can be tapped like telephone lines, with little incriminating evidence left behind. Some LANs can even be tapped from a distance, with users picking up the radio-frequency emissions that almost all LANs produce. However, this is not a common problem outside high-tech industries.

Two important security measures to prevent taps include:

- The use of fiber-optic cable. Some LAN managers are turning to expensive fiber-optic cable because it is the most tap-resistant media.

- Avoiding dial-up connections to LANs over public telephone lines.

In the era of enterprise computing, managers must also monitor connections between their LANs and other networks and computers. Indeed, security risks increase when LANs gain access to other networks. To prevent problems, LAN managers should:

- Regularly update the passwords and other security measures associated with these links

- Periodically audit access to and from network bridges, routers, and other links

What *Secure* Means

There is a problem in that *security* can be a vague term. What is considered secure in one organization may not be considered secure in another. To arrive at a definition of security for your specific LAN, your organization must first examine your current network or network plans to identify points of vulnerability. In other words, you will require a needs assessment.

The location of these points of vulnerability will depend on the work and network use patterns of every member of your workgroup. The first step in your security program, then, is to determine these patterns accurately. Methods for making this determination include:

- Written surveys
- Personal interviews
- Software that tracks network access by user

If you're still in the planning stages, however, you and your group will have to gather the same information about each independent PC user and then project hypothetical points of network vulnerability. Making projections is always tricky, especially if you haven't had much experience with LANs. Thus, a consultant may be helpful with this step.

Although every network environment is different, and specific points of vulnerability differ from system to system, you should be on the lookout for common problem areas. You should be sure not to overlook these areas in determining your own environment's particular potential weaknesses. These areas include:

- Network passwords
- Workstations and servers
- Files and programs

In practical terms, you need to look at your most important files, determine who can use them, and figure out how much damage could be caused if the wrong person gained access to them.

Securing Network Passwords

A key point of vulnerability are the passwords allowing access to the network itself or to specific resources such as particular servers, programs, or files. Passwords need to be secured. You wouldn't want strangers knowing your credit card number or your automated teller machine (ATM) codes; your passwords require similar protection. Some users make the mistake of writing down their passwords or storing them in some electronic note file. The problem is that if these users leave these notes where others can find them, you will erase all of the benefits pass-words create.

As a rule of thumb, users seem to remember their passwords better when they choose their own. These passwords need to be obscure enough so that unauthorized users would have difficulty guessing them. Avoid using obvious choices such as your birthday, telephone number, or the name of a family member.

Passwords should be selected that also have some personal signifi-cance and are easy to remember. The disadvantage of assigning pass-words randomly is that you eliminate personal significance. In many cases, random passwords are also harder to remember.

LAN management also demands implementing routines for changing passwords regularly. Some network managers automatically invalidate any password more than 30 days old. Others ask users to change person-al passwords each time they make complete backup copies of your net-work files. Managers should encourage users to memorize passwords, rather than write them down.

Securing Workstations and Servers

The most basic level of security is at the workstation level. The best way to protect against both accidental and intentional breaches of network security is for users to develop good workstation-protection habits. For example, you turn off a workstation when leaving work so the screens do not attract undue attention. Then you should lock up. Physical locks are also available for keyboards, disk drive doors, and workstations or PC system units. Don't make the mistake, however, of keeping keys to these protection devices in unlocked desks.

The line between workstation security and server security is blurred. Problems on nondedicated servers that double as workstations can spread across an entire network. In addition, dedicated servers can be mistaken for workstations, especially if a floppy disk drive, keyboard, and screen are attached.

Overall, server security is also crucial, especially when your network is critical to the success of your business. Don't be afraid to post warning signs on servers or to secure them behind locked doors, if possible. On a simpler level, you should also consider removing the keyboard from each PC-based server and storing it in a secured area.

Ironically, carelessness and not malice creates most security problems with individual computers on LANs. For example, unauthorized access by children of authorized users can be a problem. They use the system to play video games at the same time their parents are trying to do real work. Sometimes cleaning staff also bring in games and play them at night when no one else is around. Either way, however, untrained people can accidentally cause serious network problems. They can, for example, introduce viruses. Keeping these unauthorized users off the system is a good policy.

Securing Files and Programs

Network security also filters down to the level of individual files and programs. In many cases, you can use passwords at this level. However, as an added security measure, you should always keep copies of important files on write-protected software.

Removable files also present special challenges to prevent accidental or malicious erasure as well as unwanted modifications. When copies of important files are stored on easily removable media such as floppy disks or tape cartridges, you will need to restrict access to these media by using:

- Locks and keys
- Sign-in and sign-out lists
- Supervisor monitoring

You want to do everything possible to protect the files while they are in use on a network. That means studying the procedures for opening and closing files as required by both the network and application software used, then following them. You don't want to introduce unauthorized programs, such as personal software and games, onto your networks. The reality is that unauthorized programs can contaminate your network with software viruses, as discussed in Chapter 7. Sign-in sheets and supervisory monitors are security measures used to prevent these problems.

Other Ways of Securing Networks

There are other network security tricks of the trade. Consultants can help you come up with detailed plans focusing on:

- Limiting network traffic by using switches

- Limiting access by workstations or times

- Using security monitors

Encryption

Cryptographics services provide a way to transmit information across an untrusted communications service without revealing the content of the information to those who might be monitoring the line. This is becoming an increasingly important issue. Encryption guarantees confidentiality and provides proof that a transmission has not been viewed or altered.

The Internet

The use of the Internet poses special security problems. Network managers and users who are connected to the Internet need to know that they face a constant risk of penetration. *Firewall* is the term used to describe network security designed to prevent unauthorized access from the Internet into a proprietary network, such as a LAN. A good firewall should log suspicious activity and generate alarms based on what is contained in those logs.

TIP

Besides firewalls, you can bolster security through authentification cards such as Security Dynamics Inc.'s SecurID. You can also purchase network-vulnerability auditing software designed to pinpoint a network's Achilles heel before hackers find it.

Putting It All Together

Network security should prevent all unwanted results, including damaging viruses, thefts, and accidental erasures. Network administrators use a variety of hardware and software tools, including passwords and locks. Ultimately, however, individual users need to participate in security measures for them to work across a network. Network security is often only as good as your least trustworthy user.

Glossary

encryption   Putting data into a secret code that guarantees confidentiality and provides proof that a transmission has not been viewed or altered.

firewall   Network security designed to prevent unauthorized access from the Internet into a proprietary network such as a LAN.

Chapter 9

Network Application Software

Network application software is selected based on pricing and network compatibility. One of the keys to compatibility is the operating system selected. For example, some programs are DOS-compatible and others have an OS/2 orientation. You can run word processing, databases, and other applications on a LAN.

147

Pricing

Although pricing policies for network applications software vary from vendor to vendor, the most common strategy is to issue a *site license*. A software site license permits a specified number of users to run the software on their workstations.

Sometimes, network application software is sold on a per-server basis. This allows all users connected to a single server to run the software. In other cases, the temptation is to use single-user versions of applications for an entire network, with few, if any, modifications. Copyright laws, however, often prohibit such use and industry organizations such as the Software Publishers Association are becoming aggressive with prosecution.

Compatibility

Compatibility is an issue because some network application software is incompatible with some network operating systems. Network software needs to be tested with both the printer and the network operating system. Problems may require major modification to the printer configurations or to the software itself. The relationship between your favorite applications software and a LAN operating system will fall into one of several patterns:

- **Incompatibility.** Incompatible applications will not run on a network, often because the software was written to access a local PC drive and cannot recognize the existence of additional storage devices. This is usually a problem with older software created in the era before LANs became popular.

- **Network Intrinsic.** On the other end of the spectrum, network intrinsic applications typically require a specific network operating system to function.

- **Network Tolerant/Network Aware.** These software products will work on either a networked or standalone workstation. However, files created by these programs normally cannot be accessed by other network users unless each user first loads a copy of the program via their workstation disk drive. On the other hand, network-aware versions of applications software manage the individual hardware configurations and preferences of each network user. This type of software also includes special file management features protecting files from modification errors.

- **LAN Versions of Standalone Products.** Vendors often provide network versions of their standalone products to be installed on the file server so each network user can access the software and use it as a personal copy of the application.

E-Mail

E-mail is quick, easy, and paperless. E-mail users enter the text of a message they want to send into their computers and then save the file to disk. This message is then addressed and transmitted electronically to the intended recipient's "mailbox," where it waits in the computer's memory for someone to pick it up.

In short, E-mail is versatile. An E-mail message can be:

- retrieved and read directly from the screen
- edited and printed out
- forwarded to other mailboxes
- saved as a file

What makes E-mail attractive to many users is the fact that the process can be paperless. Although you can print copies, you don't need paper originals. Moreover, E-mail text can be used just like any other computer file. In other words, selected text from E-mail letters can be inserted directly into a memo, then distributed to everyone on the network who needs the information. Figure 9.1 shows the kind of information you can pass back and forth on a typical E-mail message screen.

Some E-mail systems go as far as notifying recipients that they have mail waiting by printing a message in a corner of their workstation screen. Others ask users to periodically visit their mailbox to see if they have any unopened mail waiting.

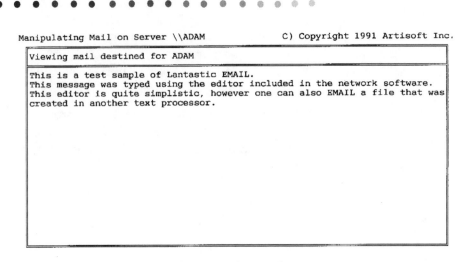

Manipulating Mail on Server \\ADAM   C) Copyright 1991 Artisoft Inc.

Viewing mail destined for ADAM

This is a test sample of Lantastic EMAIL.
This message was typed using the editor included in the network software.
This editor is quite simplistic, however one can also EMAIL a file that was
created in another text processor.

Figure 9.1 *A sample E-mail screen.*

There are three basic types of E-mail systems: external, internal, and mixed. If you have ever subscribed to an on-line service, such as CompuServe or America Online, you are already familiar with external E-mail. You can exchange E-mail messages with any subscriber to the on-line service you are using and who maintains a mailbox.

External Systems

On the other hand, MCI Mail and AT&T mail are well-known examples of external systems that service many smaller systems. These "megasystems" are maintained by vendors who provide E-mail on a subscription basis. The advantages of these systems is that they offer the ability to communicate with individuals connected to other networks. For example, you can use CompuServe to access MCI Mail and exchange messages, not only with any CompuServe member, but with a member of any network who subscribes to MCI Mail.

Internal Systems

Popular examples of internal E-mail systems include Lotus Development's cc:Mail, Microsoft Mail, IBM's PROFS, and Digital Equipment's ALL-IN-1. An internal system is designed to enable work groups within an organization to exchange messages. The trend is for internal systems to have links into external systems as well.

Mixed Systems

Many companies create systems that use a combination of internal and external E-mail systems. Analysts predict that companies using internal E-mail systems will likely increase their simultaneous use of external systems when the CCITT X.400 standard (discussed in Chapter 5) gains widespread acceptance. This standard will allow internal system users to transmit messages to subscribers of an external system without worrying about problems caused by proprietary message protocols. In 1993 a popular word processing program, WordPerfect, began to offer E-mail features that are as easy to use as printing a document. Subsequently, several other applications programs followed suit, with the result that sending electronic messages from within applications can be as commonplace as choosing **Send** or **Print** from the File menu. All that's required for the document, spreadsheet, or chart to be delivered over the network is that you add the recipient's network name or address when prompted. The E-mail standards needed for mixed systems made this kind of application-level E-mail possible.

The most sophisticated systems can convert E-mail text to voice. This capacity allows network users the ability to request that their messages be read back to them. E-Mail users who frequently work off-site use this service to play back their E-mail messages. They access their E-mail mailboxes via telephone. This feature is not yet common on PC LANs.

Databases

One of the most common reasons organizations invest in LAN technology is to enable people to share a central database. That is why many vendors are focusing their attention on LAN database management. Most of these systems use multiple file servers, allowing LAN users to share data files while, at the same time, using a variety of "locks" or controls that are designed to restrict access and maintain the integrity of the data. Several different styles of locks are used, including:

- read-only lock

- file/write lock

- record lock

While a read-only lock allows many users to look up information in a database, it prevents users from changing any part of the database file. In other words, anyone can view a read-only file, but only those people with write privileges can make changes to that file.

On the other hand, a file/write lock is placed temporarily on an isolated file or files. A file/write lock will work like a read-only file for anyone trying to get access to the protected file except the person who first queried it. The user is thus protected from anyone else interfering with their file while they are working on it. No two users can have access to the same record at the same time.

A record key ups the ante and forbids anyone else from writing to or reading from a selected file while the lock is in place. Only the person who places the lock on the file can remove it; the lock can remain in place for as long as the user chooses to leave it there. A file with a record lock, then, can be considered the most secure.

Operating Systems and Database Software

The problem with running older-style database programs on DOS-based networks is that the software running on the local workstation cannot process the data while it is physically resident on the server. All processing has to be done after copying massive records—literally entire databases—across the network to the local workstation. This approach tends to create heavy network traffic loads, which slows down long inquiries.

In an effort to overcome the slowness of working across a network, client-server systems have been developed in which much of the preliminary processing is done locally. The server-directed processing is not only kept to a minimum, but can also be done across the LAN link, without the necessity of downloading entire databases. Central to this development has been the refinement of a special kind of database query language, called *Structured Query Language*, or SQL (usually pronounced *Sequel*).

SQL

Most of the emerging database server applications are based on SQL, a language with a long history in the mainframe and minicomputer worlds that is now becoming a dominant force in PCs. The nice feature about SQL is that users do not have to understand it or even know that it is being run to use it. SQL is usually incorporated within other application packages, such as databases, spreadsheets, and even project management programs, and automatically comes into play when you start manipulating your data. For example: in a database containing all relevant statistics about the Presidents of the United States, you might want to pull out just the names of the ones born in January, or just the ones who liked vanilla ice cream. The strength of SQL as a database tool is that it lets you correlate information and combine data searches in completely customized ways. Its strength as a LAN tool is that it can be used at the workstation for designing queries, which are then sent over the network to the server. The data processing is done on the server and the results of the query are sent back over the network to the individual workstation. Instead of incurring a heavy network traffic burden in downloading and uploading entire databases, network traffic is restricted to brief, speedy messages. Database updating is similarly efficient and economical since the master files always reside on the server, and any updates you make are instantly available to anyone else working on that database at the same time as you. The language enables network users to collect data through English-like statements even while working in other applications, such as spreadsheets.

N O T E   In the client-server environment, a user runs an application which interfaces with a database management system engine running on a server. The link between the programs on these two computers is a piece of software called an *Application Program Interface* (API), which is provided by the database management program vendor. SQL is supposed to provide a standard interface to data on other computers, but for a long time vendor cooperation was less than enthusiastic. Many felt that they had more to gain by maintaining their proprietary methods than by providing a common interface. However, today there are a number of SQL products that go by the sobriquet of *middleware* and allow users to access any SQL server from a variety of front-end applications.

NOTE

Microsoft has introduced the Open Database Connectivity (ODBC) standard, and Borland has developed its Integrated Database Application Programming Interface (IDBC). Both of these are intended to make it possible for just about any front end to access just about any engine and are spurring an even greater boom in SQL-based client/server application development.

LAN-Based Fax

Another trend that has developed at about the same time as the rise of SQL is that of the facsimile servers, called *fax boards*, which put the power of a fax machine inside a PC. International Data Corporation projects that the installed base of fax boards will increase from the 1990 figure of approximately 63,000 to just over 600,000 by 1994. This will greatly increase the potential for LAN-based faxes.

FAX servers also have several disadvantages that must be considered before one is selected:

- With few exceptions, fax servers are more effective at sending messages than they are at receiving them. Unless LAN users periodically check the fax server itself or are notified by the system's supervisor, they have no way of knowing when a fax message arrives for them.

- Keeping track of outgoing faxes is also difficult. A LAN manager typically has no effective way of knowing who is sending out fax messages, making cost allocation difficult. The failure to provide adequate accounting data will mean that the fax server can be abused by employees who could anonymously transmit long documents.

- Routing is a problem. While some manufacturers have introduced servers that are said to include the capability to route incoming faxes directly to their recipients anywhere on the LAN, this feature often requires specialized capabilities in the LAN operating system. It may also require that the sender use a fax board or fax machine compatible with the recipient's fax server.

Word Processing

Most popular word processing software vendors offer network-compatible versions. The network versions include file locking features designed to prevent files from being overwritten when two users have simultaneous access to a single file. From the user's point of view, however, the network version of a word processing program is virtually identical to the standalone version.

Networks demanding a large volume of word processing files often use LAN products known as *document managers*. High-end managers can handle thousands of files. These packages facilitate network user searches for word processing files by criteria such as:

- author name
- title
- subject

Other Programs

In addition to word processing programs and databases, LANs can also be used for other advanced applications, including accounting program spreadsheets and various graphics programs.

DOS and OS/2

The most common operating system, DOS, is among the least suitable for networks. It carries by far the largest body of fast-running software, however, and has been used by LAN vendors so that it will operate properly on a network.

One of the best ways to make DOS run more effectively in LAN situations is to employ a DOS Extender, and one of the best DOS extensions is

Quarterdeck's DESQview X. This software allows a user to farm out computer tasks to unused remote computers in the network. This distributed processing support even allows multiple monitor windows on the master PC.

OS/2 is a newer, more powerful operating system for PC-type computers. Developed by IBM to be capable of dealing with larger blocks of memory and to handle several tasks simultaneously, it is ideally suited to networking. OS/2's main problem is that it is just now starting to gain mass recognition and may be passed over by a user rushing to use Microsoft Windows. While Windows now comes in versions capable of operating effectively over networks, such variants as Windows for Workgroups represent products that have been retrofitted to add LAN capabilities. WindowsNT, on the other hand, is an OS/2-like operating system specifically designed for networking; it will probably become a standard, both on the basis of its own merit and because of Microsoft's marketing clout.

In general, you should not consider switching from DOS just because you are considering LAN installation. However, you should consider installing a DOS extender such as DESQview X if the idea of a single user farming out processing jobs seems appealing.

Groupware

While many people seem to disagree on a precise definition, groupware is an application of LAN technology that has been the focus of steadily increasing attention during the past few years. Basically, *groupware* is a term used to describe a set of E-mail-based tools that support collaborative work. By allowing workgroup members to share files and information, groupware is seen as improving the efficiency of information sharing and supporting the goals and objectives of a work group. Groupware is noted for its interactive and interpersonal features.

Following are three examples of current groupware functions:

- A company subscribes to an on-line news service and wants each day's news items sorted according to categories before being forwarded to selected lists of employees. A groupware product automatically scans each news item, then collects all the news items into categories that can be distributed.

- A company needs to schedule frequent meetings of employees, all of whom have different schedules. The company uses groupware that enables the company's secretary to access the public calendars of each employee. The same groupware can present overlay calendar pages of those employees who will attend the next meeting.

- Employees within a department frequently produce documents collaboratively, but have trouble keeping track of revisions. They use groupware to track additions and deletions to the text and to allow users to insert comments into them.

Many of the largest development groups have entered the field. AT&T offers Rhapsody, client/server-based workflow automation software. Lotus Development Corporation's Notes has been a mainstay of the category since the designation first arose. Version 2.0 offers improvements in terms of interface, imaging, security, applications integration and remote communications. Schedulers abound on the list of groupware.

Buyer's Guide: E-mail

Keep in mind the following considerations when purchasing E-mail software:

1. Does the E-mail package come with custom notification? All E-mail packages alert you to incoming messages, but the most flexible packages allow you to customize the notification options.

2. Does it use folders to foster organization? Look for programs that file messages in folders, instead of those that store all messages in a single list. Folders make it easy to track correspondence and archive messages. You should also look at the criteria for searching single or multiple folders.

3. Does it have an undelete utility? Programs with a message undelete feature give you a second chance when you accidentally delete messages. Unfortunately, you can't rely on the DOS UNDELETE command to do the job.

Artisoft LANtastic-Compatibility Guide

Most software is LANtastic-compatible. If you are not sure about a specific software product, you can download and review Artisoft's bulletins:

- on your fax machine by contacting the Artisoft Facsimile System at (602)884-1397.

- on Artisoft's own Arti-Facts BBS (602-884-8648). The BBS is 1200-9600 baud, 8 data bits, 1 stop bit, No parity, full duplex

- via **GO ARTISOFT** forum on CompuServe.

The following products are Artisoft LANtastic compatible and have been tested for compatibility with the LANtastic Network Operating System v4.x, v5.x and v6.x.

Accounting Software

- AccPac Plus v6.1A/LanPak 6.0A and accounting modules—Computer Associates

- AccPac BPI CPAC BPI Integrated Accounting version 4.0a and LanPak version 4.0a—Computer Associates

- Levinson Lyon Business Accounting Systems v2.12.1—Charter House

- PAS III v3.1, Client Accounting v3.1, MPM v1.03 and DBD v1.03—CYMA Systems

- Peachtree Complete Accounting v8.0—Peachtree Software Inc.

- Peachtree Accounting for Windows Release 3.0—Peachtree Software Inc.

- Simply Accounting v2.0—Computer Associates

- Unilink Write Up*Plus v6.1—Unilink

Backup: Hardware and Software

- Cheyenne ARCsolo for Windows v3.0—Cheyenne
- Interpreter PLUSseries TapeXchange v5.1—Interpreter Inc.
- Jumbo 120, Jumbo 250 and QFA 700—Colorado Memory Systems
- Maynstream for DOS v3.1—Maynard (division of Archive)
- Maynstream for Windows v3.1— Maynard (division of Archive)
- Nsure v1.20—FortuNet, Inc.
- Sytos Plus for DOS v1.32—Sytron Corp.

Bulletin Board Systems (BBS)

- The Major BBS v6.11—Galacticomm, Inc.

CAD Software

- AutoCAD 386 release 12—AutoDesk

Database Software

- Alpha4 v2.1—Alpha Software Corp.
- Dataflex v3.01b—Data Access Corp.
- dBASEIV v1.1—Borland International/Ashton-Tate Inc.
- Lotus Approach for Windows v2.1—Lotus Development Corp.
- Paradox for Windows v4.5—Borland International
- Q & A v4.0—Symantec Corp.
- R:BASE v4.5—Microrim, Inc.

Desktop Publishing

- Harvard Graphics v3.0—Software Publishing Corp.

Disk/File Utilities

- CacheAll v1.0—C&D Programming
- Norton Utilities v6.01—Symantec Corp.
- PowerSync for Windows v1.11—Linkpro, Inc.

Fault Tolerance Subsystems

- Immunity Disk Mirroring Software v1.x—Unitrol Data Protection Systems, Inc.
- No*Stop Network v3.0—Nonstop Networks Limited

Fax and Modem Sharing: Hardware and Software

- EZ-FAX v3.52—Calculus, Inc.
- JetFax II with JFDos v5.x and JFWindows v2.x—JetFax, Inc.
- Nuko Information Systems MessagePort v1.5—Nuko Information Systems, Inc.

License Management Utilities

- AppTrack v1.0—C&D Programming

Miscellaneous Hardware and Software

- GPIBridge v1.1—PC Support
- ITSFile Document Imaging family of products—Information Transfer Systems, Inc.
- Silver Streak Ethernet Network Connector AUI model—Tut Systems Inc.

Multitasking/Windowing Software

- Windows v3.0x—Microsoft Corp.
- Windows v3.1x—Microsoft Corp.
- OS/2 Version 3—IBM Corp.

Operating Systems

- MS-DOS 5.0—Microsoft Corp.
- MS-DOS 6.0—Microsoft Corp.
- MS-DOS 6.2—Microsoft Corp.
- DRDOS 6.0—Novell, Inc.

Personal/Workgroup Productivity Software

- Angoss v2.52A—Angoss Software International
- CCMail v4.02 for DOS and v2.0 for Windows—Lotus Development Corp.
- Freelance Graphics for Windows v2.0—Lotus Development Corp.
- Futurus Team v2.02—Futurus Corp. (also compatible with the Artisoft Sounding Board)
- InForms v1.0—WordPerfect Corp.
- Instant Recall Office v2.0—Chronologic Corp.
- Notes v3.0—Lotus Development Corp.
- Ontime v2.2, Ontime for Windows v1.25—Campbell Services Inc.
- Organizer v1.11 for Windows—Lotus Development Corp.
- The Meeting Room v1.0—Eden Systems Corp.

Remote Access Software

- EXAC v1.42—3rd Planet Software
- Stampede Remote Office v1.2—Stampede Technologies, Inc.

SNA Gateway Products

- SNA LAN Gateway v2r2—Eicon Technology

Spreadsheet Software

- Lotus 1-2-3 release 2.3 and 2.4—Lotus Development Corp.
- Lotus 1-2-3 release 4.01 for Windows—Lotus Development Corp.

Uninterruptible Power Supplies (UPS)

- Back UPS, Smart UPS—American Power Conversion
- Tripp Lite BC/LAN, Omni/LAN—Tripp Lite

Vertical Market Applications

- Builder Information System v4.01—Management Information Control System
- DogDoc v7.7—Sinclair-Dow, Inc.
- Eclipse v6.0—MPN Software Systems, Inc. (HNA Computer Systems, Inc. Distributors)
- Point v3.2A—Calyx Software
- Sketch Library v3.6—Apex Graphics Systems

Word Processing

- AmiPro v3.0—Lotus Development Corp.
- Word for Windows v6.0—Microsoft Corp.

- WordPerfect v5.1, and WordPerfect v6.0 for DOS—WordPerfect Corp.

- WordPerfect v5.2 for Windows—WordPerfect Corp.

- WordStar 6.0—WordStar Int'l Corp.

For further questions about the Artisoft LANtastic Compatibility Program, please call the Artisoft Compatibility Department at (602) 690-3300.

Putting It All Together

LAN analysts predict that, as organizations move from a single-user orientation to a network-based approach to office computing, you will see more and more software products designed to increase workgroup productivity. The most obvious of these products are E-mail and group schedulers. Image databases, central fax servers, and shared accounting databases will also become common features in companies.

Glossary

Application Program Interface (API)	A piece of software that links two other programs.
e-mail	Paperless, electronic messages entered at one computer and delivered over a LAN to the addressee by specialized communications software.
fax board	The modem part of a fax machine that plugs into a personal computer. It generates signals directly from computer files or the screen and transmits images the same way.

groupware

A set of E-mail-based tools supporting collaborative work and improving the efficiency of information sharing, supporting the goals and objectives of a work group.

site license

A contract to use software within a facility, providing authorization to make copies and distribute them within a specific jurisdiction.

Standard Query Language (SQL)

A standard language for accessing databases.

Chapter

10

LANS and Electronic Imaging

Electronic imaging is a term used to describe software and hardware for capturing and holding records in electronic form.

Why Is Imaging Popular?

One of the key reasons people turn to electronic imaging is its efficiency. By eliminating paper shuffling, electronic imaging systems save time. Information industry estimates show that a typical worker in a typical department, such as accounts payable, will take 12 minutes to process a document. Nine of these 12 minutes will be spent searching for, retrieving, and refiling the document, as opposed to the three minutes actually spent processing it. Electronic imaging systems eliminated most of those nonproductive operations. Misfiling is also a problem. Industry experts estimate that the average cost of a misfiled record has climbed from $74.15 in October 1975 to $126.81 in June 1991. Electronic records can also be misfiled, but at least the computer can help you look for them.

When you consider that American businesses generate more than 2.7 billion sheets of paper that go into file folders every day, you can easily see why the cost of processing documents is staggering. The companies involved in producing the technology, equipment, systems, and supplies for the creation, use, storage, and retrieval of information account for almost half of the Gross Domestic Product of the United States. That is why most analysts see the electronic imaging industry as in the middle of a boom cycle.

Image-Based LAN Applications

Image files are usually much larger than other types of data. Text, for example, occupies little space (e.g., a single 3.5 inch diskette can store 1.4 MB of information, or approximately 5,000 pages of text). The same floppy might hold a single gray-scale image.

Fortunately, new software and hardware developments have made image transmission possible. Compression software has greatly reduced the amount of storage space required for images. In addition, new optical discs have increased storage capacity. A 5.5-inch optical disc stores 600 megabytes of information. That's the equivalent of about 200,000 pages, or more than 1,500 conventional 5.25-inch diskettes. Twelve-inch optical discs, which store as much as 800,000 pages of text, are readily available, as are 14-inch disks capable of storing about 7 GB of information. The most commonly used optical disc in imaging systems is the WORM (write once, read many) disc. In 1992, re-recordable magneto-optical drives began to appear.

Storage is further enhanced by optical jukeboxes, which operate much like musical jukeboxes (via robotics) to service businesses with extremely high-volume storage requirements. These units can store more than one terabyte of information on multiple optical discs and permit users to access any or all of them interchangeably. LAN-based image applications fall into two general categories: *indexing* and *workflow*.

Indexing

Indexing applications usually involve the storage and retrieval of large quantities of images. For example, banks frequently use LAN-based indexing applications for image-assisted signature authorization and verification. Banks store images of check authorization documents for each of their corporate clients and signature cards for all employees authorized to sign checks. When a bank employee needs to verify a signature, he or she calls it up on the LAN workstation. The advantage of this system over looking for a signature card in a paper folder or on microfilm is that saves time. Not only is locating the signature easier, but refiling is simpler.

Workflow

Workflow applications, on the other hand, require an image system to be integrated with other existing LAN applications, for example, image-assisted design change processing, a system often used in manufacturing. First, design change packages containing relevant drawings and related documents are scanned into the image system. Once the drawings have been approved, they are stored in the image servers and made available to all authorized network users. The review process is controlled by electronic routing slips that automatically circulate the documents and provide the tools needed to approve and forward them.

A Brief History of Image Systems

The first imaging machines were customized products from systems integrators. FileNet Corp pioneered the concept of turnkey imaging solutions. Today about 20 firms offer imaging systems; a number of vendors, however, have created special LAN-based image systems, including:

- IBM
- FileNet

- Wang
- Hewlett-Packard
- LaserData

In the beginning, vendors first developed special, proprietary network architecture. Today, however, more companies are taking an open approach to imaging technology. More and more vendors are producing systems that perform image functions on existing equipment currently used for other applications. Today, most analysts agree, the network itself is no longer a critical factor in determining the performance of a LAN-based image system. The data speeds of today's Ethernet and Token Ring LANs are more than adequate to handle image traffic.

Using Multiple Servers

Even today, however, most LAN-based image processing systems use multiple servers. Each of these servers performs a specific image function. A common configuration will include:

- a large file server to store the images that everyone will view
- a print server dedicated to complex graphic printing
- a high-speed fax and modem server that everyone on the LAN can use to access

A typical LAN-based image application will use most, if not all, of these servers. A document request goes to the database server. This server returns a result set listing the documents that meet the criteria indicated by the request; the user then selects a needed document. This document is transferred from the optical server to a magnetic storage buffer on the file server's hard disk and is routed to the workstation where the image is decompressed and displayed.

LAN-based image system performance is determined by the following:

- workstation characteristics
- network interface cards
- video adapter cards

The workstation in a LAN-based image application must perform the process of image decompression. This process requires powerful computing resources. At a minimum, a computer planning to run extensive image applications should have a 386 (or above) processor and run at a clocking speed of 33 megahertz.

A 10-megabit-per-second Ethernet LAN is the minimum speed recommended for imaging applications. Video adapter cards, on the other hand, determine how fast an image will be transferred from the workstation memory to the screen. You will need a high-speed video card for workstations used primarily for image processing, preferably one with a graphics coprocessor.

Desktop Video

Video applications are on the cutting edge of LAN applications. The specific capabilities of these technologies will vary greatly from vendor to vendor. The most advanced systems have multiple capabilities and use windows to display the different types of information being processed simultaneously. These elite systems make it possible to deliver analog video, such as cable network or satellite broadcasts, to each LAN user's workstation. LAN-based video products enable network users to conduct conferences that can include:

- full-motion digital video
- digital audio
- data from the network's database
- images from the image server

In most cases, however, LAN-technology is not quite that sophisticated. In 1993 Microsoft introduced *Video for Windows*, which allows many Windows word processors and databases to add short video and sound clips to their documents. Serious users of desktop video will need at least a 486 computer with a minimum of 8 MB of RAM and a 200-MB hard disk drive.

Video conferences are also promoted by the use of LANs. Some systems allow users at either end of the conference to edit information by entering spreadsheet data and by drawing on photographs and images. Some of the products used limit videoconferences to a particular LAN.

Some, called *point-to-point systems*, go as far as limiting the conference connection to two sites. Other multipoint systems make it possible to include several LANs or even wide area network participants.

Imaging and LAN Software

Kodak, IBM, Novell, and Lotus are working on software to further the migration of imaging systems from the mainframe to LANs. Lotus, for example, has incorporated imaging into its Notes groupware application. Notes users can capture images with scanners and place them directly into documents created with word processing, spreadsheet, and graphics programs. Figure 10.1 shows a typical flatbed scanner; Figure 10.2 shows what a typical handheld scanner looks like. They can also include the images in E-mail. Lotus has worked with Kodak Desktop Document Imaging group, which has developed imaging equipment and standards that are being licensed to a number of vendors. IBM has integrated imaging into OS/2. Novell's Image Enabled NetWare is a set of components providing document imaging capacities on NetWare networks.

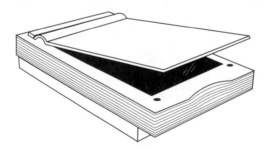

Figure 10.1 *An optical scanner.*

Figure 10.2 *A handheld scanner.*

Imaging Standards

In many cases, the technologies used are based at least in part on the IEEE 802.9 draft standard for integrated voice and data LANs. The Standard 802.9 specification:

- defines the use of twisted-pair wiring
- defines an ISDN-like transmission plan for the local area
- designates a packet channel for data applications
- designates a circuit channel for voice and digital video

Networking CD-ROMs

You can share CD-ROM drives on a network three ways:

- Allow users to access the drives located on workstations in peer-to-peer environments. Windows for Workgroups and LANtastic allow access to the CD-ROM drive in the same way as any other drive.

- Install CD-ROM drives in the file servers, then install appropriate drivers to make that drive available to network users. For example, if you are using Novell NetWare, the *NetWare Loadable Module* (NLM) called CDROM.NLM is the driver that provides the support for mounting CD-ROM drives.

- Create a dedicated CD-ROM server and install appropriate drivers.

CD-ROM SERVERS

The rise of systems using CD-ROMs also is accommodating the trend toward imaging LANs. (CD-ROM stands for *Compact Disc-Read Only Memory*.) The CD-ROMs that computers use store digital data and are similar to the CDs you see in record stores, but have a slightly smaller capacity. Numerous organizations use networked CD-ROM systems to distribute a range of stored data including:

- engineering specifications
- computer system documentation

- demographic data
- financial profiles
- multistate telephone directories

Many LAN analysts predict that the convergence of high-capacity storage systems, such as CD-ROMs, and high-speed transmission technology will allow networks to eventually become multimedia communications and distribution systems.

The primary advantage of CD-ROM technology as a network resource is its large storage capacity. Each CD-ROM disk can store approximately 650 megabytes of data, in formats including:

- ASCII text
- computer code
- numeric data
- scanned images
- digitized audio

CD-ROM software also provides powerful cross-referencing search features, facilitating the use of the technology as an ideal database medium.

Meanwhile, while many of the technical issues associated with CD-ROM networking are answered, thanks to software development questions regarding pricing and licensing still need to be resolved. For example, many publishers of CD-ROM databases have not yet established policies for using their products in a multiuser environment such as a LAN. Some charge a base price for the database and charge additionally for each workstation. Others require users to purchase additional copies, instead of allowing multiple access to the same database.

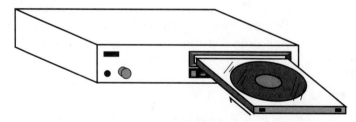

Figure 10.3 *Typical CD-ROM drive.*

Putting It All Together

Electronic imaging and LANs are two growing technologies influencing each others' development. Imaging system are growing, thanks to a desire for more office efficiency and the new breakthroughs in storage technologies. Imaging systems also promote better customer service and interoffice communication. Many imaging systems are turning to LANs because they are cost-effective.

Glossary

compression	The act of reducing storage space for data.
computer-aided design (CAD)	Using computers to design products.
Compact Disc-Read Only Memory (CD-ROM)	Discs that store compact digital data.
decompression	The act of taking data with reduced storage space and returning it to its normal size.
dots per inch (dpi)	A measurement of screen or printer resolution.
electronic imaging	The process of capturing, storing and displaying visual information not already in electronic form.
gray scale	A series of shades from white to black.
halftone	The simulation of continuous-tone images, such as shaded drawings and photographs, with groups of dots.
indexing	Organizing information for search and retrieval.
line art	Scanned images treated as black-and-white points.
NLM	A driver (specialized software) designed specifically to support one particular function on a Novell NetWare LAN.

optical juke box   An automated device for housing and reading many optical discs.

pixel   A dot.

point to point system   In videoconferencing, a session limited to two sides

raster graphics   Resembles television, where the picture image is made up of dots.

terabyte   One trillion bytes.

throughput   The combination of processor performance, data transfer and memory access.

vector graphics   Maintains the image as a series of points, lines, arcs, and other geometric shapes.

workflow   The automation of a set of standard procedures, such as records management, by imposing sequential rules until they are completed.

Write Once, Read Many (WORM)   A digital storage medium on which information can be recorded only one time, but read indefinitely.

Chapter

11

Reconsider: You May Not Need a LAN After All

Sooner or later, most organizational PC users consider a LAN. What they are looking for, primarily, is a way to share disk space and printers.

Along the way, many of them end up checking out alternative ways to reach the same goals. Some settle for other solutions, at least temporarily.

Although a LAN will deliver more benefits than any lesser solutions, sometimes you may want to consider an alternative. At times the main purpose of a LAN, which is the sharing of computing resources, can be reached by ways that are less expensive or easier to operate. Indeed, these "babystep solutions" may be a first step toward full-blown LANs.

Sharing Storage Areas and Programs

The earliest and simplest system, often known as "Sneakernet," is still in widespread use today. With this system, you save a file from one PC on a floppy disk and take it to another PC where it is loaded again. (Presumably, you will be wearing sneakers when you do this. You could also wear loafers and do the same thing, but "loafernet" probably doesn't have the same pizzazz.)

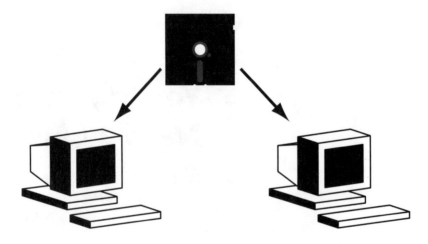

Figure 11.1 *"Sneakernet" is nothing more than carrying your disks from machine to machine.*

The rise of inexpensive portable computers with 100 megabyte hard drives (often selling for less than $1000) has helped give Sneakernet a new life. Many users write and do calculations "on the run," save their work on disk, then transfer their files to an office or home-based PC. Sneakernet works best where:

- Almost everyone uses the same type of PC disk drive, and
- Ease of file sharing is more important than applications such as E-mail.

Otherwise, Sneakernet has some basic problems. You can't always take a floppy from one PC and insert it into another PC. Sometimes you run into problems such as:

- **Platform Incompatibility.** You can't always transfer a Mac file to a DOS computer and vice versa.

- **Media Incompatibility.** You can't put a 5.25-inch floppy into a 3.5-inch drive.

- **Application Incompatibility.** Although great improvements have been made in this area, even today, many applications will not recognize or translate all of their fellow programs.

In the past, one way to get around hardware and software incompatibility while manufacturers worked out all the translation issues was through the use of software/cabling packages, which were products designed to make file transfers easy, even among machines with incompatible disk drives. The packages include a length of cable that plugs directly into a port on each of the two computers and include popular conversion utilities. Among the more popular brands are the most recent versions of LapLink for Windows, Traveling Software, and DataViz's MacLink Plus PC.

Despite its effectiveness, many users find this sort of transfer solution slow and inconvenient. Vendors have also provided MS-DOS add-ons and cards that achieve true MS-DOS compatibility, running Macs as actual 386 or higher PC-type machines. In addition, many Macs equipped with the Apple Super Drive can now read and write PC disks. Some, such as the Power Mac line of Macintoshes, can run DOS and Windows programs while simultaneously running Macintosh programs. However, not everyone wants the hassle of learning two operating systems and wildly dissimilar software. Also, this solution is more expensive than buying a PC clone.

Working with Apple File Exchange (AFE) Files

Today there are simpler software-based solutions, particularly file-translation software, that will change whatever you've got into whatever you need. These solutions have short learning curves. In many cases, you can just use a **Save As** button on your software that lets you save your files in whatever format you choose. Apple also has worked to make translation possible with its FDHD SuperDrive and Apple File Exchange (AFE) software. The SuperDrive that comes with every new Macintosh can read MS-DOS floppies, but the Mac's System software cannot. Instead, Macintosh System software comes with AFE, a utility that lets you look at the contents of a DOS disk and copy a DOS file to a Mac disk.

Many users find the interface for the AFE utility hard to use. Another problem is that you don't get many options with AFE. It does work well with several programs, however, including: ProDOS (Apple II) files and word processing programs written in Document Content Architecture/Revisable Form Text files (DCA/RFT) and MacWrite.

Meanwhile, other software developers have worked to improve upon AFE. For example, Systems Compatibility Corporation has released SoftwareBridge for the Macintosh, a series of AFE extensions that make possible a wider range of translation and which you can adjust to meet your own translation needs. Other developers have also developed utility programs that allow users to see and use floppy disks with the intuitive and very familiar Mac Finder. For example, both Access PC from Insignia Solutions and DOS Mounter from Dayna Communications will read floppies from a variety of sources, including:

- A SuperDrive
- An external MS-DOS floppy drive
- Removable media devices
- Erasable optical drives

POWERPC

The newest attempt to ease translation problems between Macs and PCs is a feature included on some of the PowerPC-chip-equipped Power Macintoshes. These machines have a new RISC-based processor as their central processing unit (CPU) and, since the chip was jointly developed by Apple and IBM (among others), the principle of file sharing has been an important consideration from the most basic level of development. Many Power Macs come with a set of programs, called SoftWindows and SoftPC, that let you open Windows and DOS files directly in a separate window on the Macintosh desktop. This solution lets you keep copies of your PC software on your Mac. You can run your Windows and DOS programs, access your Windows and DOS files, and (if you feel the need) save them from PC format to Mac format, all from a single location. Power Macs are expensive machines, however, and choosing this solution just for the sake of avoiding a LAN might wind up costing you more than it would be worth.

A Note on File Translation

The problem with file translation programs is that they need constant updating because software programs are constantly being updated. Just as surely as Word 1.05 gave way to Word 3, 3.02, 4 and then 6, there will one day be a Word 7, 8, and so on. Each time a new version of a popular program is released, the value of a translator like Software Bridge or MacLink Plus PC is diminished, until their programmers can come up with the key to the new formats. As long as we use different computers with different programs on them, there will be a need for translation software.

Portable Solutions

Electronic storage space can also be shared without the benefit of a LAN. Many manufacturers offer portable, external hard disk drives that can be used with one computer and then moved to another computer and used with it, as shown in Figure 11.2. Of course, the two systems have to be compatible and use a compatible interface.

Figure 11.2 *A portable hard drive.*

You can also get small hard drives capable of fitting on IBM PC-compatible expansion cards, complete with the necessary controller circuitry. These can be used for file sharing among computers. One drawback, however, is that having to open and close computers and insert and remove the drive cards can be a nuisance.

A variant of the portable hard drive is the cartridge drive popularized as the *Bernoulli Box*. These, along with various other removable high-density magnetic, magneto-optical, and writable optical disks provide virtually limitless drive space. They also let you carry disks, drives, or both from machine to machine to share files and programs as needed.

Printer Sharing

In the past, many organizations first became interested in networks after they bought their first laser printers. At the time, laser printers were a major investment. Even today, with fine printers selling for as little as $500 to $1,000, many firms are trying to figure out ways to share these resources efficiently.

In some cases, a LAN makes sense. However, there are also several simple, low-cost printer-sharing approaches that might be more appropriate for any organization that really doesn't need a LAN. One of the most economical solutions is a mechanical *switch box*: a device that plugs into the printer and into the PCs that will be sharing it. You can have a switch box outlet for each of the PCs. Each outlet (A, B, C, etc.) would be marked on the switch box. The user of the PC connected to switch box outlet A would turn the switch to the position marked A, which would send a file to the printer. As soon as computer A's print job is finished, the user of computer B or any other computer could turn the switch to position B and begin printing. You can also get electronic versions of the switchbox. They eliminate the need to get up and walk over to the switch each time a print file is sent. These devices also automatically eliminate the power spike problem sometimes found with manual switches. Electronic switches monitor each connected computer and automatically establish the printer link when a print request is detected.

Buffers

You don't want to use switch boxes, however, in offices that churn out documents almost continuously. Productivity will wane while people wait their turn to print. The more practical solution under these situations is a buffered printer-sharing unit. A buffer is a block of built-in memory for storing incoming print files. Should the printer be busy, users can transfer print files to the buffer and move on to their next task. They don't have to wait until the printer is free because the queued files normally are printed out in the order they are received.

Most buffered-printer sharing devices can be attached to a range of products capable of handling between four and ten PCs. Sometimes, these devices allow several computers to share one printer. In other cases, the devices themselves can be linked together to increase overall capacity. When you are evaluating at buffered printer devices, be sure to study:

- memory size
- cabling requirements

In many cases, the buffer will store about 100 pages in text. Standard memory on most of these units is 256K. Most vendors also offer memory upgrades.

You can use buffers whether you share printers or not. If you are using your equipment primarily to turn out word processing text, look for a printer with at least a 64K buffer. If you use desktop publishing, you'll need at least 1Mb.

Ports and Cabling Requirements

The type of port, or connector on your PC, will determine cabling requirements. There are two types of ports:

- parallel
- serial

A parallel port sends or receives all eight bits of a standard computer word, (byte) simultaneously over eight wires. The resulting data transfer is, therefore, 8 times faster than transmission over the serial port, which sends bits one at a time, or "serially," over a single wire. However, any device connected to a parallel port needs to be in close proximity to the PC for it to work. If you use a parallel port, you will probably have to locate your PC within 20 feet or so of your printer.

A device connected to a PC via serial connection, on the other hand, can work when it is far away from the printer. Figure 11.3 shows examples of parallel and serial cabling. You can connect a printer to a serial port that is as much as 100 feet away.

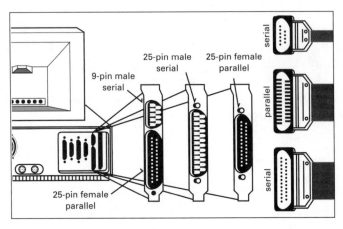

Figure 11.3 *Parallel and serial cabling.*

Multi-user Systems

A multi-user system is a single computer with multiple keyboards and screens. These systems function like many LANs, but differ in their implementation. Like LANs, some multi-user systems require a terminal on every user's desk. Each terminal, in turn, is connected to an expansion card located with others in a central chassis. Each multi-user system card holds the equivalent of a PC's central microprocessor and some related chips. The PC chassis, on the other hand, contains the system memory and provides access to printers and other shared resources.

Advantages of this type of system include:

- LAN-like appearances
- Potentially higher speeds than LANs
- Inexpensive implementation

The easiest way to think of a PC on a multiuser system is that it has literally been cloned. The clone parent stays on your desk. The clone child is down the hall. The potential advantage of multiuser systems over LANs is that the only thing broadcast to the user is the screen image, not the bulk programs or the data.

TYPES OF MULTIUSER SYSTEMS

Multiuser systems include PC-PLUS (Alloy Computer). Instead of a network operating system, PC-PLUS comes with Network Executive software that works with the host computer's copy of DOS to provide needed additional features. Alloy offers a version of Network Executive software that runs some versions of Novell's NetWare LAN operating system.

UNIX-based systems are widely regarded as being enormously suitable for multi-user connectivity. The operating system was originally designed to be very efficient at allowing several different operations to go on simultaneously. Its critics claim, however, that it is poorly understood by the average user and requires a much larger investment in time to learn it and use it to its fullest advantage. Then, too, applications programs that run under UNIX are quite often very different than those that you can buy off the shelf at your local computer store. And because of the generally low level of interest to date in UNIX-based systems, finding people who know how to install, run, and maintain the systems, as well as those experienced in using UNIX-based software are all factors that need to be weighed when you find yourself intrigued by UNIX's offers of higher raw speed.

Integrating LAN Alternatives and LANs

In the end, LANs often can be integrated with their alternatives. However, this integration requires careful matches between available alternatives and current needs. LAN alternatives must be examined carefully to ensure that they support sufficient growth, enhancement, and interconnection so that they have a future.

Putting It All Together

Because cost is a consideration causing organizations to seek ways to better their return on investments for computing equipment, they will be exploring a full range of resource-sharing options. In many cases, LANs will be the optimal choice. However, in other situations, alternatives will work better.

Glossary

Bernoulli Box	High capacity drive using removable disk cartridges.
buffer	A small memory bank used for a special purpose.
Central Processing Unit (CPU)	The "brains" of a computer. The microprocessor chip that performs the computational functions.
parallel port	Also called a line printer (LPT) port, a connector normally used for printers. A parallel port runs up to 50,000 characters per second on a PC.
port	A connector on the back of a system unit used to attach a peripheral device, such as a printer.
serial port	Also called communications (COM) port, a connector that is used to hook up printers and other devices, such as modems, communicating back and forth. A serial port runs up to 10,000 characters per second on a PC.
switch box	A device that allows sceveral PCs to share one printer.

Chapter 12

Beyond LANs

Computer connectivity is one of the most crucial issues facing the electronics and communications industries, if not our society, today. LANs are only the beginning of the tip of the iceberg. You will probably want your LAN to be connected to other computer systems. This chapter looks at the technologies and systems that make this possible.

Wide Area Networks (WANs)

From a user's point of view, a WAN appears as one large network. In fact, a typical WAN consists of a number of geographically dispersed workstation clusters, each with its own file server. The servers, in turn, are linked. That way, each WAN user can access all the resources associated with all the servers.

The individual LANs inside the WAN networks are usually referred to as *subnetworks*. They are connected by various means, including:

- telephone lines
- the use of packet-switched networks
- fiber-optic cable
- microwave transmitters
- satellite links

Metropolitan Area Networks (MANs)

MANs are bigger than LANs but smaller than WANs. Like a WAN, a MAN will extend beyond the confines of a local area network. However, it will not spread over as wide an area. As you would expect, a MAN is usually limited to a single city. Obviously, a typical MAN does not usually require long distance telephone communications. MANs have their own standards: the IEEE 802.6 standard specifically addresses MANs.

Internetworks

An enterprise network may also link LANs, WANs, and MANs, into a single *internetwork*. The most well-known example of an internetwork is *Internet*. Initially, it consisted of three large government networks:

- ARPANET—Department of Defense
- MILNET
- NSFNET—National Science Foundation

These networks span the world and connect to other private and educational networks. Since its inception, however, the Internet has grown to include literally thousands of network sites, many of them run by private individuals, all tied together into a vast global information web that can be used by any and all, for the price of a phone call. The list of Internet services has also grown. What was once a largely academic and research environment has grown to become the basic medium of computer communication for thousands of businesses and tens of thousands of individuals.

The Internet

The Internet is a global web of interconnected computers and computer networks integrating LANs located in schools, libraries, businesses, hospitals, federal agencies, research institutions and other entities into a single global communication network. The underlying connections include:

- dial-up telephone networks
- satellite links
- microwave links
- ground-based microwave links
- fiber-optic networks

The Internet is so vast that it cannot be mapped at any one time because new computers and networks are constantly being added. Electronic pathways for information are constantly changing.

The Internet grew out of the US Department of Defense project, the Advanced Research Projects Agency (ARPANET) created in 1969 and dismantled in 1990. The National Research and Education Network (NREN) is the backbone data network of the Internet. The National Science Foundation administers it.

The key to Internet interoperability is the Transmission Control Protocol/Internet Protocol (TCP/IP). The TCP/IP protocol was first used on the ARPANET, but is now available to almost every computer system as either a built-in feature or as an option that you can add.

Every computer on the Internet has an unique name and numeric address. Computers notice the numeric addresses, people work with the names. All Internet addresses have two elements:

```
local@domain
```

The domain name becomes part of every host address on your TCP/IP address. It usually has one of three suffixes: .com for a commercial organization, .edu for an educational institution or .gov for a government organization. There are other suffixes, but these are the ones you'll likely encounter most often. For example, let's make up a college named Joe Levy University. The domain would be Joelevy.edu. Every department within the school could have a local address. For example, the accounting department could be acct.joelevy.edu and the football stadium football.joelevy.edu.

LOGGING ON

Telnet is the protocol or command that enables remote logons to the Internet. The command is available on every system using TCP/IP. Some systems use the *rlogon* command.

T I P

To log onto hosts with a logon command:

1. Type **telnet** followed by the name of the host you want to logon to.

2. (Optional) If you don't type the host name, the Telnet prompt appears and you can type help to display information about using the command.

3. Once connected, type a logon name and password.

4. (Optional) If this is the first time you have logged on, get an account by typing **newuser**.

5. Once you are logged onto the system, type **help** for guidance on future commands.

If you are connected with a service provider such as America Online, you would follow their commands to navigate the Internet.

America Online, for example, offers Internet access through its Reference area.

Services Available on the Internet

Once you are on the Internet you are ready to browse around or use various services. Popular services include:

- electronic mail (E-mail)
- chat services
- news
- file transfer
- world wide web

ELECTRONIC MAIL

Electronic mail is probably the most active service on the Internet. The Internet uses a communications method known as the *Simple Mail Transfer Protocol* (SMTP) which lets users send messages. With an SMTP-based mail system, a PC user can send and receive messages with users anywhere on the Internet without going through a special gateway to translate messages.

If you want to use the Internet's E-mail services you can turn to many sources, including:

- GEnie—a popular service provider with mail exchange services for the Internet
- CompuServe—a popular service provider with mail exchange services for the Internet
- MCI Mail—a mail delivery service provided by MCI Corp
- BITNET (Because It's Time Network)—A dialup UNIX network
- FidoNet—a dialup DOS network
- UUCP (UNIX-to-UNIX Copy protocol)

Because privacy is important on a network—the Internet is adopting *Privacy Enhanced Mail* (PEM) standards. PEM provides confidential and authenticated E-mail using public key encryption methods, coded symbols, such as *9! or &^%. The mail is electronically signed by the sender using these encryption methods. The receiver can then verify the signature using public keys.

CHAT SERVICES

Chat services are real-time communications sessions you have with one or more Internet users at the same time. During a session you can type messages that other participants see and read their replies—or you can just sit back and watch the conversations of other users. Sessions take place in special forums related to topics such as health, finance, aviation, computers and many others. You can use chat as an interactive one-to-one communication service or as an IRC (Internet Relay Chat), an interactive many-to many service.

USENET NEWSGROUPS

Usenet is a group of systems for exchanging information. It is like a bulletin board or conferencing system with ongoing topics and postings anyone can respond to. Categories include news, science, recreation and other topics. There is no central Usenet authority. Usenet users include government agencies, businesses, and home users.

FTP

FTP is a program for transferring files in TCP/IP environments such as the Internet. In most cases, users download files, including text or graphics, from a remote server. You use FTP to connect with another system and execute various commands for listing files and transferring them between systems. A session will begin by typing *ftp* at the command. Following are some commonly-used commands:

- **Help** to display a list of help commands
- **dr** or **IS** to list files in the remote system's directory
- **cd** directory name to change directory
- **cdup** to move up a directory
- **pwd** to display the current directory name
- **get filename** to copy a file from the remote system to your computer
- **put filename** to send a file from your system to the remote system
- **bye** or **quit** to end the session.

WARNING

Files are transferred in ASCII format unless you choose a different transfer mode. Type **binary** before typing the **get** command to transfer a binary file.

INFORMATION DISCOVERY SERVICES

Fortunately, navigating the Internet is much easier than you might imagine. Here are a few of the more popular discovery services:

- **Archie** is a service enabling you to locate information on anonymous FTP hosts quickly. Archie tracks over 1,000 hosts and can be accessed via E-mail or Telnet. Archie sites include archie.ans.net (New York) and archie.unl.edu (Nebraska)

- **Wide Area Information Service (WAIS)** has servers maintaining indexes of Internet documents. It is a search-and-retrieval service helping you refine future searches.

- **Word Wide Web** provides information discovery services using hypertext links among documents.

T I P

The World Wide Web is an increasingly popular tool for electronic publishing. It uses the Internet as a platform for documents containing text, graphics and links to other databases of information. Many online services and Internet providers support Web access.

The Cost of Moving Up and Out

If you are considering linking your workstations, via your LAN, to the great world beyond your doors, there are some special preparations you need to make to ensure successful connectivity.

Internetworking Hardware

The most important pieces of internetworking hardware are bridges, routers, gateways, and backbones.

BRIDGES

A bridge will connect two similar networks at the data link layer of the LAN's architecture. The primary function of a bridge is to transfer data signals, or packets, from one network to another. It also amplifies the signal, thereby performing the function of a device known as a repeater.

Many bridge systems today use a process known as *filtering* to determine whether the data packets being transmitted are intended for a separate network. For example, if the workstation on a LAN issues a message intended for a workstation on another LAN, the bridge will:

1. Read the destination address included with the data packet

2. Determine that a bridge between the two LANs is required to complete the communication

This feature reduces the excess traffic on the other LAN and replaces the older systems that automatically send messages from one network to another.

Bridges encourage the division of large LANs into subnetworks. Subnetworks offer several advantages, including:

- **Enhanced LAN performance.** Overall network performance decreases any time new devices are added and the cabling medium is stretched. Subdividing a network enables fewer network devices to make demands on a given segment of a network cabling system.

- **Increased network security.** You can keep different types of data with different security considerations on physically separate media.

- **Increased network reliability.** A fault on one part of a large network can disrupt communications among all connected devices. Problems on a subnetwork will affect only the subnetwork where the fault is located.

Bridges can connect LANs that use different media such as twisted-pair and coaxial Ethernet. The biggest drawback to using a bridge, however, is that it cannot translate data between different network protocols.

CONNECTING BRIDGES

There are basically two types of bridges: *full* and *remote*. The type of bridge system selected will depend on how much distance there is between the networks to be connected. LANs located far apart would probably require remote bridges and would be connected by telephone wire. Two networks located within a limited geographic area, such as separate buildings in a plant, would be connected with a full bridge.

ROUTER

A router provides the filtering and bridging functions of a bridge. It operates at the Network layer of the LAN's architecture and is often built to be protocol-specific. Routers can be made to analyze traffic conditions on the LAN and implement route-selection and traffic control features. They work like a switching station in a train yard: a signal from a foreign network arrives at the router and is stored there until all previous packets have been handled. The router then determines the packet's destination address. It looks up that address in a built-in routing table, which lists:

- the various devices on the network
- the paths between those devices
- the costs associated with transmitting information over those paths

The router then selects the most economical path, or arranges a data "detour" when an inoperative link prevents the data from being transmitted along the best network route. Sometimes routers will break a packet down into smaller packets to prevent distortion caused by noise on the telephone lines. Some routers also make special detours to subnetworks when traffic on one network link becomes too heavy and slows down network performance.

GATEWAYS

The purpose of a *gateway* is to connect networks with completely different architectures, such as a Macintosh LAN and a DEC mainframe system. The gateway, usually a PC with special gateway hardware and software, responds to a request for a file transfer between two such systems by accepting the file and then completing the transfer by using the file transfer protocol required by the receiving system.

Gateways require special attention so that network performance is not inhibited. In some cases, a second gateway is added for this purpose. However, a second gateway requires additional software.

The basic philosophy of networking should be, "Simplify, Simplify." PC gateways are, on the other hand, complex. They get the job done, but many LAN engineers ask, "Isn't it time we move that work to our real network servers?"

BACKBONE

Another important way to connect networks is via a *backbone*, a wire that stretches between networks. Under this system, user workstations are connected to servers, which, in turn, are connected to the backbone. In other words, an individual user is not connected to a backbone. Many backbone networks use broadband network system technology, originally developed for the cable television industry. The advantage of this technology is that it provides a large bandwidth and is capable of transmitting across long distances. Fiber-optic cables make great backbones.

Broadband communications channels are also versatile. They can be divided into subchannels. A typical broadband application today can share data signals with other forms of electronic communications traffic, including:

- voice
- video
- remote monitoring of gauges and controls

The major disadvantage of broadband networks is their high cost. They also require special technical expertise to run. From a technical point of view, the biggest difference between broadband technology and the more common baseband technology is the signaling technique. Baseband networks transmit data in digital form; broadband networks use analog signaling. They use modems to convert data signals to analog form.

INTERNETWORKING FACILITIES

LAN-to-LAN links also require some type of communications channel to actually carry the information. They usually operate at 5000 to 500,000 characters per second. Alternatives include:

- leased lines
- dial-up lines
- packet switching
- frame relay
- ISDN
- broadbased ISDN

Telephone lines provide one of the most popular means of connecting distant networks. In most cases, this method requires the use of a modem to convert the digital signals from the LAN into analog signals used by telephone lines.

Dedicated telephone lines can be leased to service network connections. Leased lines avoid the connection delays and other problems found in dial-up telephone line arrangements. Dial-up telephone lines, where one modem calls another and initiates an interchange, are relatively inexpensive. However, they are relatively slow, operating at no more than 2500 characters per second. Some day, the nation's telephone backbone will be all fiber-optic and coaxial connectors, allowing dial-up access at LAN transfer rates (200,000 characters per second).

Under a process known as *packet switching*, an organization can use a moderately high-speed line only when it needs data transmission facilities. In other words, companies pay for packet-switched service on a per-transaction basis instead of the flat fees that leased lines charge.

The basis of this technology is the transmission of units of data known as packets. Packet-switching systems do not use modems to move packets over telephone lines. Instead they will use a packet/assembler disassembler (PAD).

The packet switching system works like this:

- A PAD at one end of the system breaks the information into packets
- The information travels through a network of interconnected switch centers
- A PAD at the receiving end puts the packets back together

The most well-known packet-switched networks in the United States are Telenet and Tymnet.

FRAME RELAY

Instead of a separate technology, *frame relay* is a form of packet switching system. Many analysts predict that it will become a dominant LAN technology. Frame relay systems, however, are designed around digital technology. (Other packet switching system uses analog technology). Frame relay networks can assemble, route, and disassemble packets much faster than other packet switching systems. They also provide bandwidth on demand, a feature that allows a network subscriber to adjust capacity according to the type of transmission.

Because this technology is hot, several telecommunications services offer frame relay service. Several vendors have introduced frame-relay bridges and routers.

INTEGRATED SERVICES DIGITAL NETWORK (ISDN)

Integrated services digital network (ISDN) arose as part of an evolutionary trend that began in the late 1960s when Bell Telephone started phasing electromechanical switches out of central offices in major metropolitan areas throughout the country. In its place, Bell sought to promote end-to-end digital connectivity. Digital signals, of course, use binary codes to transmit information and are more compatible with computers than analog systems that try to reproduce the human voice. In most cases in the United States today, ISDN uses standard twisted-pair telephone lines to connect the telephone company central office to ISDN-compatible customer equipment. An ISDN network termination device provides the network interface.

ISDN follows two basic standards. The Basic Rate interface, which is more common in the United States, uses two B channels and one D channel. The Primary Rate interface supports 23 B channels and one D channel.

ISDN's multiple-channel design allows subscribers to conduct simultaneous transactions. For example, a Basic Rate subscriber can carry on a telephone conversation over one B channel while transmitting document images over the other.

ISDN reduces the need to maintain dedicated networks. The signaling functions performed by the D channel allow subscribers to modify their network access to meet differing communications needs and to eliminate service change delays. In other words, ISDN allows you to manage the use of the multiple bandwidths to transmit any type of data image.

The D channel also provides an automatic number identification (ANI) service. ANI prints the number of the incoming caller on a display device attached to or built into an ISDN-compatible telephone set. This service will screen calls. ANI also facilitates customer service because it can automatically access the caller's image or data files.

However, several technical glitches have slowed the pace of nation-wide ISDN deployment in the United States. These include compatibility problems, cost uncertainties, and standardization problems.

COMPATIBILITY PROBLEMS

Telephone company switches are not always compatible with ISDN adapters. This problem confuses organizations in the process of evaluating the hardware requirements of ISDN deployment. They usually buy the switches provided by their local telephone companies. Organizations, however, face problems when they try to move equipment to sites outside the realm of the local telephone company.

COST UNCERTAINTIES

Cost uncertainties result because most carriers have sold ISDN services under customized contracts. Details of these contracts have not been made available for public scrutiny. Many potential users find that without the ability to evaluate ISDN cost effectiveness, they are less likely to make commitments.

STANDARDIZATION

ISDN is becoming more standardized. Many of the larger organizations in the U.S. telecommunications industry recently agreed upon a standard that may help reduce technical confusion and cost uncertainties. National ISDN1 is an effort to implement technical specifications and agreements regarding switch interoperability developed by the network industry and the Regional Bell Operating Companies. Meanwhile, an IEEE working group is working toward developing a standard interface between LANs and ISDN.

Ultimately, the use of ISDN network interface and protocol standards, which are the same for all types of digital traffic, could significantly reduce the need for modems and other data and image conversion devices.

BROADBAND ISDN

These systems take full advantage of fiber-optic technology. In experimental wide-area networks, settings can deliver in excess of a gigabit (one billion bits) per second. One of the most prominent of these emerging systems Synchronous Optical Network (SONET), can provide data transmission speeds ranging from 51 megabits per second to 2.4 gigabits per second. A network based on SONET technology can provide a high-speed broadband ISDN network capable of transmissions of voice, data, and video.

Putting It All Together

Communication between computers and LANs is made possible by an increasing array of hardware options and systems.

Glossary

backbone   A high-speed medium linking several LANs or other computer resources.

baud rate   The number of bits—binary digits—the computer sends each second.

bridge   A device for connecting two similar networks at the Data Link Layer of LANS architecture.

digital   Using binary code to represent information.

filtering	Process of transmitting a selected range of frequencies while blocking others.
frame relay	A form of fast, digital packet switching.
gateway	a device for connecting two dissimilar networks.
gigabit	One billion bits.
internetwork	A network that connects networks.
metropolitan area network	Like a WAN, only smaller.
Packet Assembler/ Disassembler (PAD)	Equipment used to move packets over telephone lines.
packet switching	A process for moving information.
Privacy Enhanced Mail	Standards for providing confidential e-mail via public key encryption methods.
router	A device for connecting two LANS at the Network layer of the LANS architecture.
Simple Mail Transfer Protocol	The internet's electronic mail protocol.
subnetwork	A LAN that is part of a larger network, such as a WAN or MAN.
TCP/IP	The Internet's communication protocol.
Telnet	The protocol or command that enables remote logons to the Internet.
wide area network	Geographically dispersed workstation clusters, each with its own file server.

Chapter 13

A World Away: Remote LAN Access

Back before I started making my living from a freezing garrett, I used to travel. A lot. And since I was overall head and final sign-off person for six different departments, I found myself spending most of my road-time talking on the phone with several assistants and trying to sort out questions like, "who-has-what-and-when-do-I-get-to-look-at-it-before-it-goes-to-whom." Another time, I worked for a blithering drone who liked to mention casually at 30,000 feet that he expected to see the finalized personnel evaluations (or quarterly budget analysis, or some such) on his desk the day we got back to the office. All of the relevant files, of course, were locked up in a database on my desktop machine and by no means finished, because this same boss thought it was really neat to yank me along whenever he felt like his Samsonites were getting a wee bit lonely there in the back of his closet.

The Problem

If you're fortunate enough not to hear an echo of your own travails in any of this, try a couple of these scenarios on for size:

- You keep telling yourself that someday you're going to get home in time to finally see your children awake so you can find out the color of their eyes. Seems like every time you try to leave work at a decent time, though, the backlog on your desk grows just a little more. You could use a way to access your LAN from home, so you wouldn't have to haul a bunch of disks back and forth and then spend time updating the office version of your files after you've spent your evenings and weekends getting your work done.

- You're wasting too much valuable time when you're on the road. You must have current information from the company database before you call on your clients. But since that information can change quickly, and without notice, you're spending more time calling headquarters, talking to your assistant, and copying numbers into your laptop's version of your database than preparing yourself for other aspects of your client visit.

- You're part of a project team and want to keep track of—and contribute to—development work on the new widget, or program, or campaign. Simultaneously, you also have to host a panel discussion at a convention out of town.

There are more scenarios, but by now you see the common thread. You need to be two places at once. You need access to your programs back at the office and you need the ability to make meaningful updates to work in progress. This is something that can't be handled by an E-mail connection, either. Getting messages is one thing, and enormously valuable in its own right, but what you need is the ability to reach out and actually do some work when you're far from the friendly confines of the corporate HQ.

The Solution

These are situations where remote-access software provides exactly the kind of long-distance bit-bashing capability you need. If you've never heard about this before, it could make your life a lot less frazzled. If you've heard about it, but shied away because of a healthy fear of losing your soul to modem-communications voodoo, now may be the time to look more closely. The software has been around for a while and has improved with age. There are a number of these remote access programs on the market. Most of them appear to be quite good, and they're not all that much of a mystery to use successfully.

What are They?

Basically, remote-access packages are programs you can use to connect via modem to your office PC or local area network. Alternately, you can use them to directly connect two adjacent computers by means of a simple serial cable and null modem. The software comes in two parts: a Remote component that you install on the PC you take with you; and a host component you install on the desktop machine you leave behind (or have your network administrator install on your LAN's gateway computer).

In the case of your desktop machine operating as a host, you leave the system on when you're away and, by dialing in through a modem, your laptop or remote desktop machine acts as though it were simply an extra keyboard, mouse, and monitor attached to your office-based PC. In network-access situations, the host/gateway is a modem-equipped PC which acts as a conduit for remote machines into your office LAN. Once your remote computer connects with the gateway, you have all the same LAN capabilities you'd normally possess. It's just as if you were back at your desk, the only difference being that your physical location is irrelevant. Whether you're working from home or from a hotel room in Jakarta makes no difference. The LAN sees you as though you were in your office.

Close-Up

Norton-Lambert's Close-Up is one example of a remote window onto your PC or LAN. With it, you can directly connect two PCs, connect your laptop or remote PC to your desktop PC, or connect your laptop or remote PC to your office LAN. The same program runs under either DOS or Windows, comes on a single 3.5-inch disk, and sets up in a matter of minutes. The installation program automatically loads each computer with both host and remote capabilities. You can call into your office PC when you're at home or on the road, or turn around and call your home PC if you get to work and find you left a file at home and don't have the time to commute back to pick it up.

When you load and run **Close-Up** from Windows you actually go through a Windows-to-DOS-to-Windows transition. Start out by clicking on the Close-Up icon in Windows. The program drops you into DOS for dialing and connection to the host. If the host is up and running Windows, Close-Up acts as though it was another Windows application on the host. If the host is running under DOS, Close-Up treats your remote PC as a simple DOS extension of the host.

Close-Up also includes a number of handy and/or time-saving features that help to make your entrée into remote computing a simpler task. For example, it uses a feature the manufacturer calls *Photographic Memory* to help speed up communications when you're using it in Windows mode. As you know, Windows is heavily dependent on graphics. Graphics are, almost by definition, extraordinarily large consumers of disk and memory space. In an interactive communications environment, any constant updating of the Windows interface makes the whole process quite time consuming with anything but the very fastest computers and modems. The way Close-Up works around that is to slice up the screen and only keep transmitting the section you're working on. It holds the rest in local memory, and it can hold several different windows in memory at once. For example, if you're flipping back and forth between several different pages in a word processing document, Close-Up "remembers" each page and snatches it from local memory when you hit the **Page Up** or **Page Down** button. Close-Up only gets involved in shipping bits over the wire when you start making changes to an individual database field, spreadsheet record, or part of a document. Then, the part of the screen that actually changes is usually relatively small. By limiting data transfers over the telephone lines to those small parts of the screen that change, the whole process is speeded up, according to Norton-Lambert, by as much as 200 to 300%.

All remote access programs have a password system for increased security and a very nice feature that lets you disable the host's screen and keyboard from your remote PC. Remember, when you are communicating from home or on the road, your office PC is running just as though you were sitting there in the office. As a result, anything that appears on the screen at your remote PC is also being displayed on your office PC's screen. Similarly, both the remote and the host keyboard can be used to enter data simultaneously. You could wind up with a situation where, either by accident or design, you come on-line to the host and get the decidedly spooky experience of seeing an application-in-progress because somebody back at the office has decided to use your machine while you're away. You could simply unplug your monitor and use your key-board-lock keys to shut things down, but then somebody could always come along and plug the monitor in again and scope out your work-in-progress. Not good. Like most of the other remote control programs on the market, Close-Up also contains a general communications program that will let you connect to bulletin boards and conferencing systems.

Carbon Copy

Microcom's Carbon Copy comes in two separate versions, one for DOS and one for Windows, although the distinction is a little more subtle than it first appears. You can actually work with both DOS, and Windows applications if you have the Windows version of Carbon Copy. With the DOS version of the product you can only work in DOS but it also incorporates some terminal emulation capabilities that are dispensed with in the Windows version. The terminal emulation features of the DOS version (also found on pcAnywhere, discussed below) make it especially useful if your particular host is one of the big IBM or DEC mini or main-frame computer models.

Both the DOS and Windows versions come equipped with host and remote components, and both can be used with individual PCs acting as hosts or with gateway/hosts on LANs. Both versions also have add-on software packs for LANs that let users remotely control other LAN work-stations. This feature is used mainly by LAN administrators for such things as remotely updating other users' software. Both the DOS and Windows version sets up quickly and without asking for a lot of information from the user. The main things you have to tell it are your name, whether you are using a serial port or LAN connection, and whether or not you want the host to require a password from remote callers.

Carbon Copy is a large program, the Windows version seems to be particularly large. You'll need at least 4 megabytes of disk space for the program, plus an additional 2 megabytes as a swap area during setup, for a total of 6 megabytes of free space on the disk during the installation procedure.

There are many interesting features and cross-compatibilities that are part and parcel of the Carbon Copy products. For example, the Windows version of the remote software can also be used to call into a host that is configured with the DOS version of Carbon Copy. This way, if you already have the DOS version running at one of your company's locations, other users from different locations can call in with the Windows-equipped versions. Nice touch.

Carbon Copy for Windows operates at up to 115,200 bits per second, which is nice for direct connections, and has options for MNP-10 connections (a modem option that lets you get clear transmissions over particularly noisy telephone lines) and cellular connections. By contrast, the DOS version has a maximum speed limit of 38,400 bps and no special MNP-10 or cellular modem features.

The whole Carbon Copy for Windows user interface is button-oriented so, once you've set up a Guest-Host communications session, you can perform a lot of routine functions just by clicking on an icon. Carbon Copy for Windows also has automatic data compression and drag-and-drop features for file transfers. You get a directory tree of the hard or floppy disks on both computers and can simply look up the file you want to move, then drag it to the place you want it to go. Once you drag the file to the destination's icon, Carbon Copy compresses the file, transmits it, and uncompresses the file at the receiving end.

pcAnywhere

Symantec Corporation's Norton pcAnywhere, like Carbon Copy, comes in separate versions for DOS and Windows. Each version also has an add-on software pack for LANs that lets a user at one workstation remotely control up to five additional workstations. The Windows version comes on two 3.5-inch disks (which can be traded for 5.25-inch disks), while the DOS version comes on four 5.25-inch disks (tradable for the 3.5-inch format). With the pcAnywhere for Windows version you set your machine up to act as both a host and a remote user with a single installation. With the pcAnywhere for DOS version you have the choice of only being a host, or only being a remote user, or setting up to act as either a host or a remote as circumstances warrant. The pcAnywhere for DOS version's remote portion also lets you access a host that is running Windows, and lets you access your remote capabilities as an application under Windows. Once you load and run pcAnywhere for DOS, either from the command prompt (in the case of either host or remote) or from the Windows Program Manager (for remote only); your access to program commands is through a series of menus. Everything is neatly and logically arranged, and if you've ever used such menu-driven programs as The Norton Utilities you'll feel right at home.

The pcAnywhere for Windows interface is button-oriented but arranges things differently from the way Carbon Copy for Windows does it. For example, in Carbon Copy one of the buttons that's always available on the screen is labeled *Chat*. Push the button and you can hold a typed conversation with a user at the other end. The button is active even if you happen to be off-line at the moment. Pushing Chat when you're not hooked into another computer yields a message dialog stating that the button is currently inoperable. pcAnywhere also has a Chat capability, but the button is unavailable until after you've made a connection and then call up a separate on-line menu. This two-tiered menu structure separates the actions you can perform while communicating (such as Chat, Save Screen, File Transfer, End Session, etc.) from the things you do in order to set up or configure a communications session (Be A Host, Call a Host, Call an On-line Service, Exit). The main setup screen also contains a menu bar with all the selections you need to set up your PC and modem for any type of communications session.

ARA

The big name in remote access for the Macintosh is Apple Remote Access, or ARA, and comes from Apple Computer rather than from a third-party software developer. As with the Windows and DOS remote access programs, ARA is a true blessing when it comes to getting meaningful work done on the office LAN while you're stranded in the airport at Timbuktu. ARA provides you with a door into your office machine or your office LAN and, once connected, the user interface is indistinguishable from any other Macintosh LAN connection.

In fact, ARA operates so transparently that there's not a great deal to say about it. You sit down at your remote Mac, launch the ARA application, and when the connection is established, proceed with your work just as if you were back in your office. Its ease of use can make it a little tricky, though. Don't be fooled into thinking that just because you can navigate your LAN effortlessly from a remote site that you'll have all speed you'd normally expect. As with any kind of communications connection, either PC or Mac, the pipeline you're pushing bits through is very, very small. Serial communications over telephone lines is much, much slower that the 10 Mbits per second you can expect out of most LANs. Even with a fast modem you will be better off if you connect to the office LAN for simple things, like checking your schedule, picking up your mail, and uploading or downloading files than trying to do useful work on server-based application programs. It is possible to run a spreadsheet or query a database through the telephone lines, but as a practical matter, the process is so slow you'll be pretty disappointed with the overall results.

Scripts

A major concern for anyone using remote access software is the problem of trying to keep the expense to a minimum. Long distance phone connections are expensive and working remotely can be horrifically time consuming, with correspondingly horrific phone bills. This is where scripts come into the picture. *Scripts* are canned sets of instructions, like macros or batch files, that you prepare beforehand and then run while on-line. If you habitually perform the same actions, like downloading a weekly report or checking your on-line mailbox, using a script to automate these actions is one way of saving yourself the time and trouble of going through the motions manually. It's faster, since the computer can perform the actions faster than you can, and the computer generally makes fewer typing errors. Using scripts also means that you don't have to be anywhere near the computer to get some work done. Set up a script to dial the phone at two in the morning when phone rates are low, download the file, and hang up when finished, and you can be sleeping at home while these operations take place.

Caveats

All of the convenience, utility, and freedom notwithstanding, remote computing is slower than sitting down at your desk and tapping away at your own keyboard. How much slower depends on the hardware and software you're using. In remote computing, speed is a variable over which you have a very large degree of control, depending on the equipment you use.

On the whole, if you need to be two places at once and your name doesn't happen to be St. Anthony (a medieval cleric famous for just such a trick), a modest investment in any of these programs will pay handsomely. Just make sure you have fast modems at both ends and a comfy spot to work from at home.

Putting It All Together

Remote access gives you another way of using your LAN. With remote LAN access you can work on your office LAN from home or while away on business. The current crop of software available for remotely accessing your LAN is both reliable and fully featured.

You will need to develop personal procedures and work habits that let you make the most efficient use of remote access software. Once you become comfortable with working remotely, however, you will be able to work efficiently and conveniently from any location.

Glossary

remote-access   Programs you can use to connect via modem to your office PC or local area network. Alternatively, you can use them to directly connect two adjacent computers by means of a simple serial cable and null modem.

scripts

Canned instructions for automating routine actions, like downloading a weekly report or checking your on-line mailbox, using a script to automate these actions is one way of saving yourself the time and trouble of going through the motions manually.

Appendix

User Groups and Other LAN Resources

If you are looking for information about how to use your PCs better, the best place to start is with a user group based on the hardware or software you are using. The best place to find such a group is to review listings in the Encyclopedia of Associations. To get this book, check your local library or write:

Encyclopedia of Associations
Gale Research
835 Penobscot Building, Detroit, MI 48226

Among the many computer groups you will find listed are:

- PC Hackers

- Digital Equipment Computer Users Society

- Special Interest Group For Computers and the Physically Handicapped

- International Association of Computer User Groups

- Desktop Publishing Applications Association

- National Epson Users Groups

- Networking Institute

Your vendor retailer may also have contact information for groups meeting in your immediate area. Indeed, almost every major city has a PC user group whose members meet regularly to exchange information.

User groups have members at all levels of expertise. In other words, you don't have to be intimidated by the prospect of joining one. All of the group's members were once new users too. Most would love to have you join and will make you feel at home. If you have any questions, a member will probably have the answer or can point you in the right direction.

Membership fees tend to be low. In exchange you will receive at least some of the following:

- Monthly or weekly meetings

- Conferences attended by vendors who show their latest wares

- Newsletters that contain product reviews and tutorials

CLASSES

The best place to start your education concerning a computer product or system, such as a LAN, is frequently a course. To take courses on specific products or turn about computers, you can turn to a variety of sources, including:

- Leading retailers

- Community colleges

- Adult education programs

- America Online, Compuserve and other online services

- Schools specializing in computer education

- Four year colleges and universities

With the exception of courses held at colleges (two- and four-year) and universities, most computer courses are very short. Many last only a day or an evening or two. They tend to get right to the point and offer hands-on experience. On the other hand, college courses meet one or more times a week for several weeks. That way you can learn about a concept in class, go home and try it, and then return to the following class with your questions. In many cases you can take these courses on a continuing education basis and not worry about the stress of time-consuming, graded course work.

Novell

Novell also has extensive education programs. Novell's program consists of:

- Novell Authorized Education Center Program

- Certified Netware Engineer Program

- Certified Netware Instructor Program

- Novell Technology Institute Affiliate Program

TIP Microsoft, IBM, and Banyan all have similar types of programs. The Yellow Pages of most metropolitan area telephone books are a good place to look for initial information on any of these companies and their educational organizations.

Novell Authorized Education Programs

Novell Authorized Education Centers (NAECS) are educational partners with Novell. Organizations that meet Novell's education standards are authorized to teach Novell-developed courses using Novell Certified NetWare Instructors (CNIs). These organizations include:

- distributors
- resellers
- OEMS
- consultants
- independent training organizations

For more information about the NAEC program or to locate the NAEC nearest you, call (800) 233-EDUC. Outside the U.S. and Canada, call (801) 429-5508.

CERTIFIED NETWARE ENGINEER (CNE) PROGRAM

The CNE program helps service technicians provide support for NetWare networks by ensuring that they have received extensive training and meet Novell's certification requirements.

All of the following can become CNEs:

- Technicians who work for qualified Novell resellers
- Technicians who work for independent service organizations
- Self-employed technicians
- NetWare customers

For more information on how to become a CNE, call (800) NETWARE (U.S. only).

CERTIFIED NETWARE INSTRUCTOR (CNI) PROGRAM

The CNI programs provide training through Novell Authorized Education Centers (NAECs). CNIs must go through an intensive instructor training program and can specialize in areas such as:

- NetWare
- Communications services
- Network management
- TCP/IP and UNIX connectivity

Periodic update training keeps CNIs current.

For more information, call (800) 233-EDUC, in the U.S. and Canada. Outside the U.S. and Canada, call (801) 429-5508.

Novell Technology Institute (NTI) Affiliate Program

The NTI Affiliate program provides NetWare education to institutions of higher education. NTI affiliates offer training under Certified NetWare Instructors (CNI).

For more information, call (800) 233-EDUC, in the U.S. and Canada. Outside the U.S. and Canada, call (801) 429-5508.

Bulletin Boards

Bulletin boards (BBSes) are the high tech way of sharing information. Computer bulletin boards provide users of computers with modems a way of exchanging information and posting questions. Many software and hardware companies have their own bulletin boards.

For more information about bulletin boards in your area, contact your retailer or local user group. If you want more information on bulletin boards, in general, see *Using Computer Bulletin Boards* by John Hedtke, published by MIS:Press.

On-Line Services

On-line services, such as America Online and Prodigy, are often good sources of information about computers. CompuServe is particularly good for LAN questions.

CompuServe's Connectivity Services menu includes:

- Introduction to Connectivity Forums
- Telecommunication Issues Forum
- Electronic Frontier Foundation
- Local Area Network Forums
- Modem Communications Forums

- Other/Related Platform Connectivity
- CompuServe Mail Hub

The Local Area Network Form includes:

- Artisoft Forum
- Ask3Com
- Banyan Forum
- Cabletron Systems, Inc.
- Dr. Neuhaus
- Eicon Forum
- Hayes Forum
- IBM Communications Forum
- LAN Technology Forum
- MAC Communications Forum
- Microsoft LAN Manager (MSOPSYS Forum)
- Novell NetWire (W)
- Standard Microsystems Forum
- Thomas-Conrad Forum

A typical Novell Netwire Forum will offer:

- New User Instructions
- NetWire Easy Access Software—NOVCIM
- What's New on NetWire
- Novell Press Releases
- Forums
- Technical/Product Information

- Sales and Service Organizations
- Calendar of Events
- Novell Downloads

Books and Videos

Both videos and computer books are inexpensive ways of mastering software and hardware. The advantages of videos are that while they cost the same as books, videos are easier to digest most of the time, and often are quicker to use. On the other hand, books are easier to use on-site and provide handy reference.

Most hardware and software products come with manuals. However, the consensus seems to be that most users find them hard to read and would prefer to purchase easier-to-understand *how-to* books. Many users find that these books are a good way to teach yourself how to work a particular product. For those who really want to master a topic, publishers offer intermediate level and advanced books.

Computer books can be purchased at or through the following places:

- Computer stores
- Bookstores
- Book clubs
- Book departments at general retailers
- Mail order catalogs
- On-line book stores

Of course, you probably will want to review a book by reading the table of contents and sample passages before buying it. You will also want to make sure that it is written at the appropriate level for your background and interest. On the one hand, you don't want to feel overwhelmed. On the other hand, you don't want to waste your money buying a book that tells you what you already know.

Computer Magazines

One of the best up-to-the-minute sources of information on the computer industry in general and LANs in particular are computer magazines. These magazines, which can be found in libraries and book retail outlets, contain:

- Advertisements listing the latest hardware and software products
- Product reviews
- Tutorials
- Suggestions in the form of tips

Magazines are also written for different levels. Professional magazines target people with extensive backgrounds. There are also magazines written just for novices. Before you subscribe to a magazine you should read a few issues, either buying them off the bookstore shelf, borrowing them from a friend, or using the library. That way you will find out if the publication suits your real interests as well as your level of awareness.

Appendix B details a few of the more popular LAN and general computer magazines that are available today.

Appendix  B

Computer Magazines

BYTE MAGAZINE
One Phoenix Mill Lane
Peterborough, NH 03458

The standard in microcomputer magazines. Aimed at the computer user,
as well as programmers, engineers, and designers.

COMPUTER BUYER'S GUIDE & HANDBOOK
Bedford Communications
150 Fifth Avenue, New York, NY 10011

(212) 807-8220

Magazine devoted to buyer's guides and reviews. It includes an up-to-the-
minute price guide.

COMMUNICATIONS WEEK
600 Community Drive
Manhasset, NY 11030

(516) 562-5530

DATA COMMUNICATIONS
McGraw-Hill Information Services
McGraw-Hill Building, 1221 Avenue of the Americas, New York, NY 10020

(212) 512-2000, fax (212) 512-6833

Considered by many to be the journal of record in the communications and computing industries, this monthly magazine covers both technical and marketing issues.

INFORMATION WEEK (THE NEWSMAGAZINE FOR INFORMATION MANAGEMENT)
CMP Publications, Inc.
600 Community Drive
Manhassett, NY 11030

(516) 562-5000, fax (516) 562-5474

This weekly business publication focuses on the entire information industry, primarily for the benefit of information managers. However, its information is suitable for individuals with considerably less expertise.

INFOWORLD
1060 Bovet Road
San Mateo, CA 94002

(800) 227-8365

This weekly trade paper is noted for its in-depth reviews of LAN and PC products.

LAN Magazine

Miller Freeman, Inc
370 Lexington Avenue
New York, NY 10010

(212) 683-9294

This magazine produces articles and columns addressing the needs of
LAN managers and others in both large and small organizations.

LAN Times

McGraw Hill Information Services
1900 O'Farrell Street 200
San Mateo CA 94403

(415) 513-6800

Network World (The Newsweekly of User Networking Strategies)

161 Worcester Road
Framingham, MA 01701

(508) 820-2543, fax (508) 879-3167

A tabloid-format newspaper carrying news and regular sections on data
communications, local networking, and management strategies.

PC Magazine

Ziff Davis
1 Park Avenue
New York, NY 10016

(212) 503-3500

Published twice monthly, this magazine offers up-to-the-minute coverage of
the PC marketplace. It features article on new products, product reviews
and several continuing advice columns.

PC WEEK

Ziff Davis
10 President's Landing
Boston, MA 02155

(617) 393-3700

This weekly publication features a special insert section called "Connect," which deals primarily with networking.

PC WORLD

501 Second Street
San Francisco, CA 94107

(415)-243-0500

Appendix

A Sample Request for Proposal

You may choose to follow the format that appears on the next few pages when soliciting bids from consultants and/or suppliers. It will allow those providers sufficient information to give you a thorough estimate, while it permits you to compare competitive bids fairly.

Raupeco
1234 Maxwood Circle
Indianapolis, IN

Request for Proposal/Bid

Summary: Raupeco is a rapidly growing pet food company whose specialty is dog food. The company is five years old, with 25 employees.

Yearly sales are around $15 million. The company uses individual PCs for all information processing. Macintoshes are used for design work. DOS-based PCs are used for accounting, inventory, and distribution. Raupeco is soliciting proposals for a LAN that will tie all individual PCs together to promote greater productivity.

NETWORK SPECIFICATIONS

1. The desired solution will connect 10 stand-alone PCs, of which 8 are DOS-based and two are Macintosh; a Hewlett Packard ScanJet IIc color scanner; and two Epson EPL 7000 laser printers. However, this configuration should be able to handle growth to 25 stations.

2. The central file server should be a 486-based PC, with at least 8 MB of RAM, 100 MB of hard-disk storage, and at least an 80 MB backup unit.

3. The network operating system should be from one of the top three software companies in this area and should service both DOS-based PCs and Apple Macintosh products.

4. The amount of available RAM on each network workstation should be 2 MB or more once the necessary network software is loaded.

5. Network utility software should include the following:

   - Electronic mail (internal, with voice mail and MCI Mail gateway capabilities)
   - Printer-sharing on server and all workstations
   - Remote log-in via modem
   - User front-end menu

6. Vendor should use coaxial or fiber-optic wiring alternatives for an Ethernet or Token Ring system.

IMPLEMENTATION ISSUES

1. Vendor will provide twelve hours of basic network training to three employees at Raupeco. The vendor will also give a four-

hour seminar on network usage to all employees, and be willing to provide a one-hour follow-up session if requested.

2. While implementation does not have to take place during off hours, all reasonable efforts should be made to avoid business disruption.

3. Vendor must ensure that all application software currently running on an independent workstation runs properly after the network is installed.

4. Vendor will be responsible for reconfiguring the current integrated database and spreadsheet accounting system to run in multi-user mode on four of the network workstations and moving data to the file server.

5. Vendor will provide a complete diagram of all cabling, workstations, and servers on the network.

6. Vendor will install and test network utility software that has been listed in the specifications.

7. Vendor must be able to implement the entire solution within 30 days of being awarded the contract.

8. Vendor must be willing to guarantee the installed solution for at least 90 days from the date of installation. In addition, the vendor should provide a service quote for an additional 12 months.

QUOTES

1. Each line item on the quote will need to be written and priced individually.

2. Raupeco Corporation must receive quotes by August 15, 1995.

3. Chosen vendor will be notified by September 15, 1995.

4. Vendor should provide two references that have had a similar solution installed by the vendor for at least three months.

5. Raupeco pays one-third of the agreed-upon price on delivery and setup of equipment. The remainder will be paid 30 days after implementation is completed and accepted by Raupeco.

6. Direct any questions to Russell Cann, CFO, at Raupeco Corporation.

Appendix  D

LAN Vendors

APPLE COMPUTER, INC.
20525 Mariani Avenue
Cupertino, CA 95014

(408) 996-1010

ARTISOFT, INC.
575 East River Road
Artisoft Plaza
Tucson, AZ 85704

(602) 293-6363, fax (602) 293-8065

Tech support: Use main number.

AT&T NETWORK SYSTEMS
1 Speedway Avenue
Morristown, NJ 07960

(800) 344-0228

BANYAN SYSTEMS, INC.
135 Flanders Road
Westboro, MA 01581

(508) 898-1000/(800) 828-2404; fax (508) 898-3604

BANYAN SYSTEMS (ENGLAND)
Northwood Park
Gatwick Road
Crawley, West Sussex RH10 2XN

Phone: 0293612284, fax 0293612288

IBM
Personal System Products
11400 Burnet Road
Austin, TX 78758

(800) 772-2227

MICROSOFT CORP.
1 Microsoft Way
Redmond, WA 98052

(800) 426-9400

NOVELL, INC.
22 East 1700 South
Provo, UT 84601

(800) 453-1267/(801) 429-7000, fax (801) 429-5775

Tech support: Use main number.

NOVELL INTERNATIONAL OPERATIONS
2180 Fortune Drive
San Jose, CA 95131

(800) 243-8526/(408) 434-2300; fax (408) 435-1706

Tech support: (800) 638-9273

SUN MICROSYSTEMS
Sitka Division
950 Marina Village Parkway
Alameda, CA 94501

(510) 769-9669

SUN MICROSYSTEMS, INC.
2550 Garcia Avenue
Mountain View, CA 94043

(800) 643-8300, fax (415) 960-1300

Tech support: (800) USA-4SUN

3COM
5400 Bayfront Plaza
Santa Clara, CA 95052-8145

(800) NET-3COM/(408) 764-5000

Appendix E

The Internet

An E-mail program, a PC, and a modem is all you really need to surf the net. Thanks to the Internet and its thousands of automated mail-retrieval programs, you can access free software, electronic books, newsletters, stock quotes, financial filings, and other informational documents simply by making an E-mail request. Here are 12 research areas and fun things to do using E-mail:

1. CATALOG SHOPPING

Get the *Internet Mall*, an electronic listing of books, software, toys, concert tickets, and other products available through the Internet, by sending E-mail to taylor@netcom.com. The body of the message should contain the words **send mall**.

2. MARKET QUOTES

Tired of paying big bucks to commercial services for on-line stock quotes? You can get up to five daily stock, mutual fund, money market, and commodities quotes for free through an Internet service called *QuoteCom*. To find out more, send an E-mail message to info@quote .com.

3. COMPANY FINANCES

The SEC offers free financial information about publicly traded companies through its *EDGAR* database on the Internet. Send an E-mail message to mail@town.hall.org and type the words **search EDGAR (company name) (name of filing)** in the body of the message. For example, **search EDGAR IBM 10Q**.

4. SOURCES OF GOVERNMENT INFORMATION

A comprehensive list of Internet databases can be obtained by sending an E-mail message to mail-server@rtfm.mit.edu. The text should read as follows: **send usenet/news.answers/us-govt-net-pointers/part1** and **send usenet/news.answers/us-govt-net-pointers/part2**.

5. MARKET CONDITIONS

The *Financial Economics Network* (FEN), an Internet discussion group that lets subscribers swap information about banking, accounting, stocks, bonds, options, small business, corporate finance, and emerging markets, delivers a daily report to its members that provides a market summary of 29 indices and averages. The free report includes the Dow Jones industrial average, the Standard k Poor's 500 stock index, a list of the most actively traded stocks, and changes in foreign currency prices. Join FEN by sending E-mail to editor Wayne Marr (marrm@clemson.clemson.edu).

6. STARTING OR IMPROVING YOUR BUSINESS

You can send in a question about your company, and the *Oracle*—another Internet user—will respond with words of wisdom. It's cheaper than hiring a consulting firm, and some Net veterans swear by it. For more information, send E-mail to oracle@cs.indiana.edu with a subject line of **help**.

7. INTERNET PHONE BOOK

Want to send an E-mail message to a colleague on the AT&T Mail, Bitnet, or BIX network, but don't know the proper Internet addressing format? Get a copy of Scott Yanoff's *Internetwork Mail Guide* (commonly known as the Yanoff List) by sending E-mail to inetlist@aug3.augsburg.edu.

8. News clips

The Stanford Netnews Filtering Service searches for Internet newsgroup (bulletin board) postings tailored to your specifications and delivers them free via E-mail. To sign up for the service, send E-mail to netnews@db .stanford.edu. Type **help** in the body of the message.

9. Discussion Groups

The best way to find an E-mail discussion group is to get a copy of the "list of lists," a comprehensive register of more than 800 Internet mailing lists and their sign-up instructions compiled by SRI International in Menlo Park, California. Send E-mail to mail-server@sri.com. In the body of the message, type **send netinfo/interest-groups**.

10. Web pages

Most Web pages are also available by E-mail—thanks to a computer in Switzerland. You can request Web pages by sending E-mail to listproc@wwwO.cern.ch. In the body of the message, type **www** followed by the name of the Web page you want. For example, **wwwhttp://www.biotech .ohio.edu/WebCrawler/WebCrawler/WebCrawlerExamples.html**.

11. How-to guide

Guide to Network Tools is a free sourcebook on using E-mail, telnet, ftp, Gopher, World Wide Web, and other Internet tools. It is available if you send E-mail to listserv@earncc.earn.net. In the body of the message, type **get NetTools txt**.

12. Fax service

Now you can send faxes for free to numerous cities simply by sending an E-mail message, at least to certain locations that are listed in the return message. For more information, send E-mail to tpc-faq@town.hall.org.

13. Internet Access

Internet is available from literally anywhere in the world. The following are some numbers in Asia you can use to surf the net.

HONK KONG

Commodore Electronics Limited, 2-12 Wing Kei Road, Kwai Chung, New Territories, Hong Kong

HK Internet & Gateway Service

Phone: +(852) 527-7777

E-Mail: helpdesk@hknet.hk.net

Hong Kong Supernet
HKUST Campus
Clear Water Bay, Kowloon
HONG KONG

Phone: (+852) 358-7924

Fax: (+852) 358-7925

E-Mail: info@hk.super.net or postmaster@hk.super.net
http://www.hk.super.net/~rlowe/bizhk/bhhome.html

INDIA

aXcess Online Services
Business India Information Technology Ltd.
(Head office) 3-10 Phoenix Mills Compound, Bombay - 400 013, India.
(Branch offices) Delhi, Calcutta, Bangalore.

Type of services: Value-added online services: E-mail, Newsboard, Business, DataServe

Phone: +91-22-493 7676

Fax: +91-22-493 6578

E-Mail: sharad@axcess.net.in / postmaster@axcess.net.in

Contact: Sharad Popli, Manager, Systems & Internet Services

Note: aXcess E-mail—This service connects you to people all over India.

ERNET (Education and Research Community Network)
Gulmohar Cross Road, Number 9
Juhu, Bombay 400 049
INDIA

Phone: +91 22 436 1329 (Bombay) or +91 11 4361329 (New Delhi)

Fax: +91 22 620 0590 (Bombay) or +91 11 4362924 (New Delhi)

E-Mail: usis@doe.ernet.in

INDIALINK BOMBAY
Praveen Rao, Indialink Coord. Bombay
c/o Maniben Kara Institute
Nagindas Chambers, 167 P.D'Mello Rd
Bombay - 400 038

Phone: 91-22-262-2388 or 261-2185

E-Mail: mki@inbb.gn.apc.org

INDIALINK DELHI
Leo Fernandez, Coordinator Indialink
c/o Indian Social Institute
10 Institutional area, Lodiroad,
New Delhi

Phone: 91-11-463-5096 or 461-1745

Fax: 91-11-462-5015

E-Mail: leo@unv.ernet.in

UUNET India Limited
270N Road No. 10
Jubilee Hills
Hyderabad, A.P. 500 034 India

Phone: +91 842 238007 or +91 842 247747

Fax: + 91 842 247787

E-Mail: info@uunet.in

INDONESIA

PT IndoInternet (Jakarta)

>   Phone: (62 21) 470-2889 (check country/city code)

**University of Indonesia, Dept of Computer Science,
Jl. Salemba Raya 4, P.O. BOX 3442. JAKARTA 10002
INDONESIA**

>   Administrative Contact: Rahmat M. Samik-Ibrahim,
>
>   E-Mail: postmaster@UI.AC.ID
>
>   Phone: (62-21) 727-0162

JAPAN

Info: Changing very rapidly, check with Electronic Frontiers Japan mailing list. Send the message: subscribe to: efj-request@twics.com

**APICNET (Tokyo)
APICNET Secretariat
Global Commons, Inc.
Yamazaki Bldg. 3F 2-10-18
Okubo, Shinjuku-ku
Tokyo, 169, JAPAN**

>   Phone: +81-3-3204-8104
>
>   Fax: +81-3-3202-2414
>
>   E-Mail: In Japanese: kaneko@apic.or.jp (Ms. Yoko Kaneko)
>   In English: richard@apic.or.jp (Mr. Richard M. Pavonarius)
>   Web service at URL: http://www.apic.or.jp

Internet Initiative Japan

>   Contact: Kimiko Ishikawa (Japanese), Toshiya Asaba (English)
>
>   Phone: +81 3 3580-3781
>
>   E-Mail: info@iij.ad.jp
>
>   FTP more info: ftp.iij.ad.jp:/pub/info/English for English language versions or /pub/info/Japanese for Japanese language versions

GLOBAL ONLINE JAPAN
Oshima Building 302
1-56-1 Higashi Nakano
Nakano-ku, Tokyo 164

Type of services: Full IP support, dialup (SLIP, PPP), Shell account

Phone: (03) 5330-9380

Fax: (03) 5330-9381

auto-info: info@gol.com

E-Mail: sales@gol.com or contact us at:

NEC PC VAN

Phone: +81 3 3454-6909

Nifty Serve

Phone: +81 3 5471-5905

TWICS (Tokyo)

E-Mail: burress@tanuki.twics.co.jp

KOREA

DACOM Corporation
Address: 140-716 DACOM B/D., 65-228, 3-Ga, Hangang-Ro,
Yongsan-Ku, Seoul, Korea

Types of services: Dialup Services (e-mail, ftp, telnet) up to 14.4Kbps in all cities. IP connection services through private line. 9.6Kbps, 56Kbps, 128Kbps, 256Kbps, 512Kbps, T1, E1 in all cities

Phone: +82-2-220-5232/3

Fax: +82-2-220-0771

E-Mail: help@nis.dacom.co.kr
hscho@halla.dacom.co.kr
hscho@bora.dacom.co.kr
whchang@halla.dacom.co.kr
whchang@bora.dacom.co.kr

Hana Network
Heesoo Byun (hsbyun@hana.nm.kr)
Jeyoung Park (jypark@ring.kotel.co.kr)

Phone: () 526-6983, 526-5762 (Check country/city code)

Fax: () 526-6942

gopher: //han.hana.nm.kr

ftp: //han.hana.nm.kr

KREN (Korea Research and Education Network)

Contact: Byunho Chung (bhchung@erccw1.snu.ac.kr) and Eunkyung
Kim (egkim@erccw1.snu.ac.kr)

Phone: () 880-5364, 880-5365 (check country/city code)

Fax: () 887-0130

KREONet (Korea Research Environment Open Network)
Hyungwoo Park (hwpark@garam.kreonet.re.kr)

Phone: (042) 869-1386 (check country code)

Fax: (042) 861-1999

gopher: //garam.kreonet.re.kr

ftp: //garam.kreonet.re.kr

KORNET [Commercial]
Jongseok Lee (jslee@soback.kornet.nm.kr)

Phone: 725-2733 (Check country/city code)

Fax: 730-4668

NuriNet
I.Net Technologies Inc.
Delta Bldg. 732-21
Yoksam-dong, Kangnam-ku
Seoul 135-080

Phone: +82-2-538-6941

Fax: +82-2-538-6942

E-Mail: info@inet.co.kr

MALAYSIA

JARING
MIMOS
7th Flr, Exchange Square
Off Jalan Semantan, Bukit Damansara,
50490 Kuala Lumpur, MALAYSIA

Phone: +60-3-254-9601 or +60-3-255-2700 ext 2101

Fax: +60-3-253-1898 or +60-3-255-2755

E-Mail: noc@jaring.my or mal@mimos.my

PAKISTAN

Brain Computer Services, Brain NET!!! (New)
730-Nizam Block, Iqbal Town, Lahore-54570.

Service: dialup UUCP/emails, in 3 months live Internet!!!

Dialup: +92-42-5411888 (4 Lines V.32bis)
+92-42-7830791 (Telebit PEP First)
+92-42-7832039 (V.FAST)

Phone: +92-42-5414444 (4 Lines)

Fax: +92-42-7581126

E-Mail: info@brain.com.pk

Note: Local Nodes at Lahore, Karachi, Islamabad, Sialkot & Faisalabad.

PHILIPPINES

EMAIL CENTRE
108. V. Luna Road, Sikatuna Village
Quezon City, Philippines

Phone: +632 921 9976

E-Mail: sysop@phil.gn.apc.org

Phillippine Network Foundation Inc

Phone: (63) 633-1956 (check country/city code)

SINGAPORE

National University of Singapore (SG-DOM)
10 Kent Ridge Crescent
SINGAPORE 0511

Administrative Contact: Tong, Thio Hoe (THT3)
E-Mail: ccethio%nusvm.bitnet@CUNYVM.CUNY.EDU
Phone: (65) 772-2073
Technical Contact: Liem, Chandra (CL134)
E-Mail: CCECL%NUSVM.BITNET@CUNYVM.CUNY.EDU
Phone: (65) 7722527

SingNet

Phone: 751-5034
gopher.technet.sg, ncb.gov.sg
gopher solomon.technet.sg
gopher nuscc.nus.sg

SRI LANKA

Infolabs, Information Laboritories Ltd,
9/7/A Attidiya Road, Ratmalana

Phone: 94 1 611061
E-Mail: info@infolabs.is.lk

DATANet

Phone: (94 1) 437 545/546 (check country/city code)
Fax: (94 1) 437 547

Lanka Internet Services, Ltd.
IBM Building, 5th Floor
48 Nawam Mawatha

Colombo 2
Sri Lanka

Services: E-mail, Internet, Fax

Phone: 94-1-342974

Fax: 94-1-343056

E-Mail: info@lanka.net

TAIWAN

HiNet

E-Mail: info@hinet.net

Ministry of Education
Computer Center
106 Hoping E. Road
12th Floor, Section 2
Taipei TAIWAN

Administrative Contact: Chen, Wen-Sung (WSC1)

E-Mail: ZCHEN@TWNMOE10.EDU.TW

Phone: 886-2-737-7011

Technical Contact: Liu, Zi-Di (ZL2)

E-Mail: COLOR@TWNMOE10.EDU.TW

Phone: 886-2-737-7011

Pristine Internet Gateway
3F, No. 2, Alley 2, Lane 244, Roosevelt Rd. Sec. 3
Taipei, Taiwan

Services: SLIP, PPP, and Terminal Emulation, WWW advertising space.

Phone: 886-2-368-9023

Fax: 886-2-3670342

E-Mail: robert@pristine.com.tw

Web Address: http://www.pristine.com.tw/

SeedNet

Services: Full internet access

TAIPEI Service center

Phone: (02) 733-8779, 733-6454

Fax: 737-0188

E-Mail: service@tpts1.seed.net.tw

HSINCHU Service center

Phone: (035)773311 EXT512

Fax: (035)788031

E-Mail: service@shts.seed.net.tw

KAOHSIUNG Service center

Phone: (07)339-4105

Fax: (07)339-1990

E-Mail: service@ksts.seed.net.tw

THAILAND

Asian Institute of Technology (TH-DOM)
Bangkok 10501
THAILAND

Administrative Contact: Phien, Huyng Ngoc

E-Mail: hnp%ait.th@UUNET.UU.NET

Phone: +662 516-0110

Technical Contact: Charoenchai, Pensri

E-Mail: pensri%ait.th@UUNET.UU.NET

Phone: +662 516-0110

CCAN (Computer Communication Access for NGOs)
121/72 Soi Chalermla, Phya Thai Rd.,
Rajthevee, Bangkok 10400
Thailand

Phone: (66-2) 255-5552, 251-0704

Fax: (66-2) 255-5552

Thaisarn Internet Service at NECTEC

E-Mail: sysadmin@nwg.nectec.or.th

Phone: 662 248 8007

Fax: 662 247 1335

Web service at URL: http://www.nectec.or.th/

Assumption University KSC

E-Mail: admin@ksc.au.ac.th

Phone: 662 719 1586 to 9

Fax: 662 719 1590

VIETNAM

NetNam
IOIT, Ngia Do, Tu Liem, Ha Noi, Viet Nam

Services: BBS with UUCP link (2 daily) to Internet Dial-in access, speed (84-4) 362-352/3/4 at 9600, 8N1

Phone: (84-4) 346-907

Fax: (84-4) 345-217

E-Mail: admin@netnam.org.vn

Glossary

10BaseT	The industry standard that tracks information transmissions at 10 megabits per second.
100BaseT	The industry standard that tracks information transmission at 100 megabits per second.
analyzer	Network management tool that studies individual packets.

Application Program Interface (API)
A piece of software that links two other programs.

ARCnet
A LAN that features a physical bus and logical star. ARCnet networks have user definable addresses.

ASCII
A binary code for data in communications, most minicomputers and all personal computers.

asynchronous transfer mode (ATM)
A high-speed data transfer technology used on both local and wide area networks.

attenuation
Measurement of power loss as the signal traverses the cable.

American Wire Gauge (AWG) number
Standard measurement for the thickness of electrical wires—ranges are based on the wire's diameter.

backbone
A high-speed medium linking several LANs or other computer resources.

background
A task that is running on a workstation independent of user attention and is simultaneous to foreground work.

backups
A set of disks or tapes that contain duplicate copies of your computer files.

Banyan VINES
A network operating system based on UNIX, supports a wide variety of hardware platforms, and requires a dedicated file server. VINES stands for Virtual Networking System.

baud rate
The number of bits—binary digits—the computer sends each second.

Bernoulli Box
High capacity drive using removable disk cartridges.

BNC

Connector used on coaxial cables.

bridge

A device for connecting two similar networks at the Data Link Layer of LANS architecture.

broadcasting

Sending information from one node on a network to all nodes on a network.

buffer

A small memory bank used for a special purpose.

bus

A network in which all nodes are attached to a single cable in a daisy-chain pattern.

capacitance

Usually measured in picofarads per foot or meter, this measures the energy absorbed by the cable.

Category 5

A reference to the type of twisted-pair cable increasingly used in 100BaseT networks.

Central Processing Unit (CPU)

The "brains" of a computer. The microprocessor chip that performs the computational functions.

certifying

Establishing the integrity and adequacy of a piece of cable.

characteristic impedance

Measured in ohms; a measurement of the cable's resistance to electric current at an operational frequency.

client

A personal computer that uses services, files, and applications made available by the file server.

client/server computing

Computing done in an environment where individual systems, called servers, support multiple clients, which are users' workstations.

clustered star
A topology of several stars linked together.

coaxial cable
A network wiring medium with a metal core surrounded by grounding material and insulation.

communications server
Most commonly, modems on a network are attached to a device called a communications server. A server is any LAN computer that will service requests from others for information or action; in this case, connection (via modems) to an outside network.

concentrator device
A device linking terminals and computers to a host.

consultant
Experts hired for relatively short periods to work on specific projects; paid by the day or by the hour.

contractor
An independent consultant.

cross-platform development
The process of creating programs that work identically on both Macs and PCs and whose files can be shared between users on both types of computers.

crosstalk
Measured in decibels; a measurement of the induced signal (noise) in a wire pair from another wire pair in the same cable sheath.

daisy-chain
Connecting each computer directly to one on either side so that each computer in a network is attached to the same wire.

data switch
A device linking terminals, computers, and other computer devices to a host computer. They are basically concentrator devices. A data switch has between eight and 64 ports. Each data switch has a built in microprocessor.

dedicated server	A computer without a user, set aside to run network software, providing highest-performance network-wide data storage and printing services.
deterministic access method (DAM)	A method for connecting to a LAN that uses predefined rules and conditions to assign access priority to the various devices on a network.
digital	Using binary code to represent information.
digital volt meter (DVM)	A tool used to measure the resistance of a cable or to determine continuity.
disk caching	A set of auxiliary RAM chips that are directly attached to the hard disk controller card. This cache is a temporary storage area for frequently used data, and, since information doesn't have to be sent to or retrieved from the physical hard disk, is a much faster way of accessing information.
disk duplexing	The use of two separate controllers and two separate hard disks to provide on-the-fly duplication of data.
disk server	A hard disk used to share files with several users; the precursor of the file server.
documentation	The instructions supplied with computer hardware and software.
DOS	Abbreviation for *Disk Operating System*. DOS is the most commonly used operating system in PCs.
Dynamic Data Exchange (DDE)	A Windows for Workgroups facility that allows you to insert information in your document from documents owned by other users, even if those documents reside on other network computers.

E-mail

A system to send messages among users of a computer network, or the software that supports these message transfers.

-ncryption

Putting data into a secret code that guarantees confidentiality and provides proof that a transmission has not been viewed or altered.

enterprise computing

The computerization and interconnection of office and field workers throughout an organization.

Ethernet

A LAN access method allowing connected devices to transmit randomly. However, when more than one device attempts to transmit data using this system, both devices will wait for different periods before attempting data retransmission.

expansion slot

A connection inside a PC, into which you insert a network interface card, for example. Terms used to describe the different types of expansion slots (and cards) include: ISA, EISA, MCA, PCI, VESA, and NuBus (for Macintoshes).

fault tolerance

The name given to the taking over and continuing of normal operations in the event of a primary component.

fax board

The modem part of a fax machine that plugs into a personal computer. It generates signals directly from computer files or the screen and transmits images the same way.

FDDI

Fiber Distributed Data Interface, the high-speed 100 Mbps (megabits per second) fiber-optic network the American National Standards Institute (ANSI) has developed.

fiber distributed data interface(FDDI)	The high speed 100 mbps fiber-optic network developed by the American National Standards Institute.
fiber optic	A media used for networks, using slender glass thread surrounded by cushioning and insulating material; carries network signals at very high speeds.
file server	A centralized storage device complete with software that can be accessed by several users of a network.
filtering	Process of transmitting a selected range of frequencies while blocking others.
firewall	Network security designed to prevent unauthorized access from the Internet into a proprietary network such as a LAN.
First Mail	A simple E-mail package included with NetWare 4.1.
foreground	A task running on a workstation that is the focus of user attention.
frame relay	A form of fast, digital packet switching.
gateway	A device for connecting two dissimilar networks.
gigabit	One billion bits.
Graphical User Interface (GUI)	Screen that incorporates icons, pull-down menus,and a mouse, such as those found in Macintosh, Windows, and OS/2 Presentation Manager environments, which controls access to application programs.
ground	An electrical path designed to disperse high-voltage electrical spikes, usually by routing them into the earth.

groupware

A set of E-mail-based tools supporting collaborative work and improving the efficiency of information sharing, supporting the goals and objectives of a work group.

hard costs

Costs associated with the elimination of a line item.

hard disk

A data recording medium built into a PC.

hub

A device providing a central connection point for the connecting of terminals, computers, or communication devices. LAN hubs range from simple write-management facilities to various switching devices and can serve a variety of purposes.

hypermedia

Use of text, data, graphics, video, and voice as elements in a hypertext system. With this system, all the forms of information are linked together so that a user can move easily from one to another.

internetwork

A network that connects networks.

LAN

Abbreviation for *local area network*. A typical LAN will consists of peripheral devices and computers contained in the same building, often on the same floor.

management information base (MIB)

A specialized type of database used to store network information.

message handling service (MHS)

A Novell E-mail service.

metropolitan area network (MAN)

A LAN-like network between several different buildings.

microprocessor

The heart of a personal computer, the microprocessor is a silicon chip which is wired to take its instructions from the computer's RAM chips.

mission critical statement

A management tool linking activities that make the difference between success and failure in a company with activities related to your current system.

modem

A device that takes data from a computer and translates it into a form that can travel over a telephone line or that takes electronic signals traveling via telephone and makes them usable by a computer.

monitor

Centralized workstation that assumes responsibility for network management.

monochrome VGA

Single color, or black and white monitor.

multistation access unit (MAU)

Also knows as hubs. On a token-ring LAN, a device for connecting up to eight workstations. MAUs usually have eight or 16 ports, but may have as few as two.

multitasking

The ability to do several things at once.

NETBIOS

The standard set of enhancements for IBM PC-DOS and compatible operating systems.

Netware Message Handling Services (NMHS)

An integrated system included with NetWare 4.1. It includes facilities for enhanced internetwork routing.

network interface card

A circuit board allowing a direct connection from a personal computer to a network cable.

network operating system

Special software to get computers to talk to each other.

nondedicated server	A server that can also be used as a workstation.
object-oriented programming	A method off writing programs that uses data objects, each knowing how to respond to a set of commands that can be given to it, instead of writing programs by using a specialized language, or code.
ohmmeter	Device used to measure the continuity of your cables.
operating system	Software program that your computer runs when it first starts.
oscilloscope	A graphical device that measures signal voltage (vertical axis) per unit of time (horizontal axis).
overall throughput	The combination of processor performance, data transfer, and memory access.
Packet Assembler/ Disassembler (PAD)	Equipment used to move packets over telephone lines.
packets	Segments of transmitted information.
packet switching	A process for moving information.
parallel port	Also called a line printer (LPT) port, a connector normally used for printers. A parallel port runs up to 50,000 characters per second on a PC.
passive hub	A device on a token ring network that receives signals from one workstation for forwarding on to a destination workstation.
payback period	The amount of time it takes to recoup an investment.

PCL	Page Control Language, a page description language developed by Hewlett Packard.
peer-to-peer network	A network that uses a "superstation" workstation with extra memory instead of a central server.
personal computer	A microcomputer, also known as a *PC*.
port	A connector on the back of a system unit used to attach a peripheral device, such as a printer.
PostScript	Adobe Systems–developed page description language for printers.
present value	What a future amount of money is worth today.
print spooler	Software that allows printing to take place in the background while other tasks are performed in the foreground.
Privacy Enhanced Mail	Standards for providing confidential E-mail via public key encryption methods.
Private Branch Exchange (PBX)	Sophisticated and heavily centralized telephone system.
probe	Network management tool placed on network segments to be studied, performing a monitor's function.
protocol	A set of rules that govern communication between computers.
RAM	The Abbreviation for *Random Access Memory*, the computer's electronic memory.
random access method (RAM)	A method for connecting to a LAN that allows any connected device to request access to the shared medium at any time. Most office LANs depend on random access; others are deterministic.

remote-access

Programs you can use to connect via modem to your office PC or local area network. Alternatively, you can use them to directly connect two adjacent computers by means of a simple serial cable and null modem.

Request for Proposal (RFP)

A tool for soliciting possible vendors to match a proposed solution. An RFP allows those providers sufficient information to give you a thorough estimate, while it permits you to compare competitive bids fairly.

return on investment (ROI)

A way of measuring the relative value of investments based on the current value of projected income or savings.

ring topology

A circular bus topology.

risk analysis

The art and science of weighing the benefits and costs of a decision under uncertain conditions.

ROM

Abbreviation for *Read Only Memory*, the computer's pre-programmed memory.

router

A device for connecting two LANS at the Network layer of the LANS architecture.

scripts

Canned instructions for automating routine actions, like down loading a weekly report or checking your on-line mailbox, using a script to automate these actions is one way of saving yourself the time and trouble of going through the motions manually.

serial port

Also called communications (COM) port, a connector that is used to hook up printers and other devices, such as modems, communicating back and forth. A serial port runs up to 10,000 characters per second on a PC.

server	On a network, a special computer giving users access to services such as file sharing or resource sharing.
Simple Mail Transfer Protocol	The Internet's electronic mail protocol.
simple network management	The protocol that the network management stations and various network devices use to exchange information.
Simple Network Management Protocol (SNMP)	The most commonly-implemented management environment protocol.
site license	A contract to use software within a facility, providing authorization to make copies and distribute them within a specific jurisdiction.
sneaker net	Copying information from one hard disk or floppy disk to another. This process involves physically carrying disks (presumably while wearing sneakers) from one location to another.
soft cost	Cost for intangible benefits.
Standards bodies	Groups of industry professionals who determine the methods that will be used throughout the industry, as in creating communications protocols.
Standard Query Language (SQL)	A standard language for accessing databases.
star	A network configuration where all devices have a direct path to the hub.
Storage Management Services (SMS)	An integrated system included with NetWare 4.1 to back up files across the network on both servers and workstations. SMS will back up any workstation file independent of client operating systems.

subnetwork

A LAN that is part of a larger network, such as a WAN or MAN.

Superstation

A node that shares its resources under 10Net is called a superstation. 10Net uses the NET SHARE command to show resources. It also uses the NET USE command to use a particular resource.

surface raceway

Device allowing cables to run along the outer edges of common floors covered by metal conduits attached at the room's floorboards.

switch box

A device that allows several PCs to share one printer.

symmetric multiprocessing support (SMP)

A method of boosting system performance by offloading operating chores from the primary processor to additional processors.

synchronous optical network (SONET)

A fiber optic network standard.

TCP/IP

The Internet's communication protocol. The most widely used protocol on earth. It is the standard for the Internet.

Telnet

The protocol or command that enables remote logons to the Internet.

terminal

A desktop device that usually includes a screen and keyboard like a workstation or PC, but is incapable of performing operations unless it is connected to a computer.

time domain reflectometer (TDR)

Device that measure lengths of cable and finds opens and shorts.

token

A software "flag" that manages access to a network's connecting medium.

token passing

An access method including software that manages access to a LAN's connecting medium. When a software token is passed around a network, only the device that holds the token is able to transmit data.

topology

Basic network architecture or design.

transmission control

A data communications protocol.

twisted-pair wiring

A popular and inexpensive way of linking devices in a LAN. There are two types of twisted-pair wiring: shielded and unshielded. Unshielded cable is commonly found in telephone wires. Shielded cable is more thoroughly insulated, or shielded, from electrical interference and is more reliable.

uninterruptible power supply (UPS)

System of batteries and circuits that will allow a computer to function during a power outage.

UNIX

Multiuser multitasking operating system from AT&T that runs on a wide variety of computer systems, including micros and mainframes.

utility

Also known as a desk utility, this is a software program that helps you troubleshoot, repair, and otherwise manage a disk.

wide area network (WAN)

A LAN-like network that covers a big geographic area.

Windows

An operating environment developed by Micro- soft that enables IBMs and clones to function with a graphical user interface.

workstation

A PC that grants a user access to a network. Some workstations have disk drives, others do not.

X.400   An e-mail standard designed to connect
                                   public and private systems.

X.500   An e-mail standard designed to allow
                                   users to look up e-mail addresses.

zero slot LAN   A LAN that does not require a network
                                   interface card.

Index